SOULBBATICAL

A Corporate Rebel's Guide to Finding Your Best Life

Shelley Paxton

Tiller Press

New York   London   Toronto   Sydney   New Delhi

An Imprint of Simon & Schuster, Inc.
1230 Avenue of the Americas
New York, NY 10020

This publication is a memoir. It reflects the author's present recollections of her
experiences over a period of years. Some names of individuals have been changed.
Some dialogue has been re-created from memory.

First Tiller Press hardcover edition January 2020

TILLER PRESS and colophon are trademarks of Simon & Schuster, Inc.

For information about special discounts for bulk purchases,
please contact Simon & Schuster Special Sales at 1-866-506-1949
or business@simonandschuster.com.

The Simon & Schuster Speakers Bureau can bring authors to your
live event. For more information or to book an event, contact the
Simon & Schuster Speakers Bureau at 1-866-248-3049
or visit our website at www.simonspeakers.com.

Interior design by Laura Levatino

Manufactured in the United States of America

1   3   5   7   9   10   8   6   4   2

Library of Congress Cataloging-in-Publication Data
Names: Paxton, Shelley, author.
Title: Soulbbatical : a corporate rebel's guide to finding your best life / by Shelley Paxton.
Description: New York : Tiller Press, 2020. | Includes bibliographical references.
Identifiers: LCCN 2019046207 (print) | LCCN 2019046208 (ebook) |
ISBN 9781982131333 (hardcover) | ISBN 9781982131357 (ebook)
Subjects: LCSH: Paxton, Shelley. | Women executives—United States—Biography. | Self-
actualization (Psychology) | Quality of work life. | Success in business. | Success.
Classification: LCC HC102.5.P3826 A3 2020 (print) | LCC HC102.5.P3826 (ebook) | DDC
338.7/6292275092 [B]—dc23
LC record available at https://lccn.loc.gov/2019046207
LC ebook record available at https://lccn.loc.gov/2019046208

ISBN 978-1-9821-3133-3
ISBN 978-1-9821-3135-7 (ebook)

For my parents.

Thank you for raising me to be
independent, courageous, and curious.
I know I've made you regret it on more than one occasion.

Contents

SOULBBATICAL

Introduction: Don't Read This!

Ah, a rebel after my own heart. You just couldn't resist, could you?

Well, good, because this is where the story really begins.

Soulbbatical may be a made-up word, but I promise you it's a very real experience. It has the power to transform your life, just as it did mine.

But you can't write a book with a made-up title without explaining why you made it up, right? So here goes. Initially, I mashed together the words "soul" and "sabbatical" to describe my desire to stray from a traditional career path, and blaze new trails toward understanding myself and my bigger purpose in the world. I wanted a handle that signified the depth and importance of my decision. Something that screamed, "This is different!" This is not a conventional sabbatical. It's an internal exploration of self and potential. It's about creating new possibilities, so it seemed fitting to create a new word.

It's not about leaving your job; it's about finding yourself. It's about what happens when you're ready to liberate your soul from the clutches of your ego.

I realized along the way that the essence of Soulbbatical is not a departure from the real world; it's a way of being in the real world. It's a way of creating the life you really want versus settling for what you think you should have. It's about living and leading from a place of authenticity and courage. It's about stepping into your power and leaning into your purpose in order to unleash your wildest potential. It's about becoming Chief Soul Officer of your own life and accepting responsibility for nurturing both yourself and your soul. It's about accumulating self-worth, not suffering for the sake of net worth, and profoundly understanding that these don't have to be mutually exclusive after all.

When we slow down long enough to know ourselves, align with our souls, and set intentions for what we really want, magic happens.

And massive impact. My dirty little secret (well, one of the many that you'll learn about as this story unfolds) is that I want to become an "Impact Billionaire" (to borrow a phrase from my dear friend and brilliant coach David Taylor-Klaus). Impact is the new currency for those of us who want to make a real difference in the world. So I'm declaring here that the mission of Soulbbatical is to liberate a billion souls. To start a movement inside and outside the corporate world that has each and every one of us living and leading more authentically and courageously. That has us rebelling *for* what we believe in, not who we think we should be or how we think we should look or act. Imagine being part of a soul-centered movement where more of us are creating lives and businesses we love, rooted in meaning and fulfillment.

And where we push companies to invest in developing their own souls, to reflect these same values in their cultures and leadership principles. Imagine what could happen if more companies began to cultivate cultures that recognize and celebrate employees as Human Beings not Human Doings; that flip the "time off" script from a *payoff for hard work* to a *prerequisite for smart work*; that celebrate heart over hustle. Time away is not only crucial to our mental and physical health, but to fostering creativity and innovation as well. It gives us the chance to reflect, discover, play, reinvigorate, be inspired, and find perspective—all of which can reveal ideas, connections, and meaning in a way that our day-to-day cannot. As my coach Rich Litvin loves to say, we have to slow down to speed up. How different would our lives feel if we lived and worked by this mantra?

I dream of the day when supporting radical self-care for employees is on the C-suite agenda, and company-sponsored Soulbbaticals are the norm.

Now that's fucking impact.

And I know we're not starting from scratch, you and I. We're standing on the shoulders of giants who have been modeling and magnifying flavors of this so beautifully for years: Oprah Winfrey, Arianna Huffington, Brené Brown, Marie Forleo, Simon Sinek, and Vishen Lakhiani, to name just a few.

The principles of Soulbbatical have helped me to discover and live my best life, and to become my most authentic badass self. I feel vibrant and healthy and powerful, and so fucking alive. Everything is accessible—choice, freedom, joy, love, abundance, prosperity, and success. Owning your purpose *and* speaking your truth *and* courageously creating the life you want are like rocket fuel for a kind of holistic success I never even knew was possible. Maybe you didn't either. Maybe that's why this book brought us together.

So let's back up for a minute. I've got some 'splainin' to do.

You're probably still wondering who walks away from one of the coolest jobs on the planet? Who works her ass off for a quarter of a century to become the global head of marketing for one of the most iconic brands in the world, only to *voluntarily* flip it the bird? Who leaves a lucrative executive position to become Chief Soul Officer of her own life? Me, apparently. Me and my rebel soul.

Despite the fear, uncertainty, and chorus of doubters around me, I felt an obligation to live my life with greater intention. To turn the tables and define *my* terms of engagement for however many years I had left on this planet. To chase fulfillment until I was breathless. I'm living proof that it's never too late. I left Harley-Davidson at forty-six, started my own business at forty-eight, and am writing this, my first book, to be published by the time I'm fifty. I'm not sure there's any greater gift than living life on your terms.

Of course, early on, most people (my family included) still presumed that I was going on an extended holiday, and would boomerang back to the corporate world a year later with a sun-kissed glow, an exotic lover, and a renewed hunger for daylong meetings. They also thought I was batshit crazy.

In the beginning, I had no real idea of where I was headed, or what I might find. I simply sensed there was something of tremendous value to be discovered if I was willing to take the risk. I would be like Christopher Columbus—only cuter, sailing solo, and navigating the high seas of self (arguably more treacherous than the Atlantic).

I was crystal clear on one thing at the time: I felt wildly unfulfilled. Despite the titles, money, and accolades, I couldn't ignore a deep, gnawing sense that I wasn't being true to myself. That I had lost my identity in service of my career. That with every passing day, I was dying a little bit more inside, spiraling into what felt like emotional and spiritual bankruptcy. I wondered whether success and fulfillment could coexist. Was it really possible to feel success-ful instead of success-empty? And I secretly worried about who I was becoming. Keeping up appearances was exhausting, and making me sick.

Actually, I worried about a lot of things before I made the decision to leave Harley-Davidson. The tracks that played on an infinite bully loop in my head were:

- My identity is precariously tethered to a successful career.
- I'm no one without a title.
- The things I'm supposedly good at don't make me happy.
- The things that make me happy can't pay the bills.
- I've been chasing someone else's dream all these years.
- I will disappoint the ones I love (and who love me) the most.
- I'm a fraud who will be exposed for undeserved success.
- I'll be alone for the rest of my life.
- Saying any of this out loud will make me seem ungrateful for the abundance of privilege and good fortune I've been gifted.

Sound familiar? I'll bet! Stick with me—this story is about learning to put that shit on mute (or at least turning the volume waaaaaaaay down).

Soulbbatical reminded me that I had a profound responsibility to stand face-to-face with the raw, unvarnished, fully exposed me, and acknowledge her deepest fears and desires. To embrace the discomfort of my own feelings until I stood firmly inside my own identity and story, not someone else's. And to shed the protective armor that I had so carefully curated, layer by agonizing layer.

Whatever shape that took. And wherever it pulled me. I committed to staying open. And to carrying a hefty torch into the cave so I could illuminate the experience and draw a road map—first for myself, and then for you.

Soulbbatical was a purposefully, and blissfully, unstructured concept in the beginning. It started simply as a slowing down, to heal and nurture my neglected soul. A healthy dose of luck and synchronicity also took me to some wild new places, where I did the deeper inner work of reflection. The laissez-faire of the French countryside, the magical and rugged islands of New Zealand, the zen of coastal California, and the majestic stillness of the Canadian Rockies all served as stunning backdrops for lessons I was destined to learn. But I quickly realized that no landscape holds more potential than our own soul-scape. The power of place can feed our soul, but it can't fix it. That's *our* work. The work of venturing into the dark in order to find the light, of escaping from the doing and into the being.

Soulbbatical is a very personal journey—think of it as a choose-your-own-adventure story, if that gets your blood pumping. It's most definitely not one-size-fits-all. (Scarves and ponchos have that covered.) My calling was to leave the corporate world. For you it could look very different. It might be bringing the most authentic, courageous, and healthy you to your leadership and your organization. It might be making a change to what you're doing, or the company and people you're working for, to be in greater alignment with your values and the impact you want to have in the world. It might be a commitment to prioritizing self-compassion and self-worth in the form of boundaries and balance. And it very well might be stepping into the life you've always wanted but have been afraid to create. (Yes, that one.)

I know that this can feel really weighty. It's big stuff. Hell, it's "your one wild and precious life," as the late poet Mary Oliver so eloquently reminded us. But you're not alone—I got you. And, I promise you, it doesn't have to be as hard as it may feel in this moment. As humans, we like to make things hard, or at least to believe that things have to be hard to be worthwhile. Believe me, I had a PhD in making things harder than they needed to be, and an epic list of excuses as to why it was never the right time to do the hard thing.

Of course, I'm not going to tell you that this is easy—it's not. But

I am going to tell you that it's not as hard as your ego is making it out to be (that's the fear talking). And it's exponentially more rewarding than anything you can imagine. As Warren Buffett says, "By far the best investment you can make is in yourself."

So let's do this together. I'm committed to helping you. Not just by telling my story, but also sharing reflections and questions for you to sit with, and ideas for how to set your own Soulbbatical life in motion. Think about it this way: Every badass accomplishment is really just a series of tiny steps. We recommit every morning to taking another step. And then another. Soulbbatical can be the same way—it doesn't have to be inhaling the whole enchilada at once. But, first, ask yourself this question: If I continue to live as I am now for the next three, five, ten years or more, will I be moving toward who I want to become—or further away?

If you're like I was, you're heading (maybe even sprinting) in the wrong direction because you're "should-ing" all over yourself. Convincing yourself that you *should* do this, you *should* be that, you *should* say yes, you *should* make personal sacrifices, and you *should* achieve what's expected of you. Meanwhile, losing touch with your soul, your values, and perhaps even your purpose.

I wrote this book because I was exactly where you are. Wishing someone would put an arm around me and say, "I got you." Like I'm doing now. Consider this my personal invitation to walk together toward the growth, possibility, and soul-fillment of your best life.

Starting right now.

Before you turn the page, let's get two things straight, okay?

First, we're going to dive into some deep emotional waters together. So, let's commit to being vulnerable, honest, and nonjudgmental (with ourselves and one another). Not every aspect of my story (or other stories I share) may resonate with you—that's to be expected—but I ask that you keep an open mind about what you can learn from them anyway. Defaulting to "how easy for you" or similar arguments is a cop-out if you're fully committed to doing the work of transformation.

Second, I write the way I speak—raw, from the soul, and with a fondness for the "F bomb" (among other swear words). You may have noticed a couple peppered into the Intro. If those already had you gasping aloud or dabbing the sweat off your furrowed brow with a lace hanky, then this is not the book for you. And that's okay. I'll still be championing your journey from a less offensive distance. If, on the other hand, the no-holds-barred language got your rebel all fired up, flip the fucking page as fast as you can!

Section 1:

FULFILLMENT

1.

GETTING WOKE (LITERALLY)

I knew I was in deep cosmic shit when the same nightmare ripped me from sleep, night after night, for nearly a year:

My spidey senses are raging. Something doesn't feel right. My apartment doesn't feel right. Actually, it doesn't even feel like my apartment. It's cold and dark in that terrifying something-really-awful-must've-happened-in-here kind of way. Even the signature visual pops of my favorite color, orange—the egg chair, the vintage vases, the abstract artwork on the walls in the living room—seem dull and lifeless, muted.

Am I in the Matrix? Is the Universe testing me again? Is this what it feels like right before you get murdered?

Where am I? I'm freaking the hell out.

I scan the space.

· · ·

And then I see it, out of the corner of my eye, a hallway off the living room that I know doesn't exist in my actual apartment. *What the fuck is going on?* Someone must be messing with me. I've lived in this apartment for five years! I know every nook and cranny of its barely-pushing-twelve-hundred-square-feet.

My head is screaming, *Oh, hell no!* as my body is lured down the strange new passageway until I'm stopped in front of a doorway. A doorway I've never seen before, at the end of a hallway I've never seen before. My right hand makes slippery contact with the brass door handle. I don't even know how it got there. Everything feels out of my control. I'm miles outside of my comfort zone, wishing I still had a view of the front door, my only escape route.

Am I dreaming or awake? Did I slip into some other dimension or B-grade horror flick? God, I've always hated horror movies.

The door opens to reveal an empty bedroom. At least I think it's a bedroom. Of course, I've never seen it before. (This is getting really old, really quickly.) The creak of the door reverberates in an echo chamber of wood flooring and stark walls. I grope the closest wall in search of a light switch. Nothing. My eyes are barely able to make out the vast emptiness of the space: no furniture, no décor, and no windows. A deep chill is shooting down my spine, my lizard brain's SOS.

I'm desperate to turn back, but my gaze is suddenly pulled to a thin sliver of hazy yellow light across the room, faintly illuminating a short section of floorboard. Another door? Another room? I force myself toward the light, my legs like lead.

Twelve steps. Zero breaths. Shaking, I stare at the outline of a small utility closet I've never seen before. A dim light bulb glows from the ceiling. So, who left the light on? Through the surrealism of it all, I hear my mom's voice in my head lecturing me about wasted electricity. I'm startled by something beyond the sound of my own thoughts. It's barely audible. I hold my breath and listen again. Oh my God, labored breathing and the faintest whimper. I rip open the door and come face-to-face with a neglected, malnourished, near-death dog.

Not just any dog—*my* dog.

Moka, my precious blind pug, who had been my fur baby and guardian angel for nine extraordinary years. The gentle fawn soul, wrapped in generous layers of wrinkles and rolls, who had dutifully licked the tears of illness and divorce from my cheeks, was splayed out on the floor of this closet, draped in a loose cloak of patchy skin, barely able to lift his head.

But, wait, how can this be? Moka died six years ago. I'd been there, holding his swaddled and lifeless body, sobbing on the floor of the vet's office. Wishing we could have had more time together. Or was *that* the nightmare and *this* is real? Has he actually been alive this entire time? Was I too busy to notice or remember? Did I forget about him and leave him to die alone in a closet?

It's all a messy blur.

And then I'm screaming, crying, collapsing, reaching out to cradle Moka's skeletal form. I'm whispering into his little black velvet ears how much I love him, promising over and over and over again to stay with him. Feed him. Nurse him back to life. Never leave him again.

I'm so sorry, baby . . .

I'm so sorry . . .

I'm so . . .

And that's where it ended, every single time. I would bolt up in bed, drenched with sweat and tears, struggling to make sense of this tragedy burrowing its way into my subconscious four or five nights a week.

I'd go to bed terrified and wake up feeling crucified. I'd spend my waking hours exhausted and heartbroken and questioning reality. I worked hard to keep the armor polished and intact at work, while being scared shitless to open closet doors or close my eyes at home. Petrified of discovering that I really was a careless monster, that my worst nightmare was my cruelest reality.

The details of the nightmare became tattooed on my brain with the ink of pain and needle of repetition. The location of the unknown hallway and doors sometimes varied, but a strange force always propelled me to bear witness to the same crippling end, no matter how hard I tried to resist it. No matter how much wine I drank to incapacitate it.

This went on for my entire final year at Harley-Davidson. (Yep, you read that right.) This wasn't a quickly passing phase that six-year-old impressionable me went through after watching my first horror flick behind my parents' backs. This was a forty-six-year-old badass career woman being held hostage by a nightmare and the overwhelming shame it caused.

You know those moments in life when you (wrongly) think no one could possibly understand what you're going through, and if you dare say it out loud everyone will think you're one-flew-over-the-cuckoo's-nest crazy? This was one of those for me.

I should admit here that I did break down and confess this to my sister, Christy, over the phone after a few months, while I was racing to the bottom of another bottle of New Zealand Sauvignon Blanc after work, trying to numb the ache of endless meetings, politics, and reorganizations. (I'm guessing this may sound familiar to you, my friend.)

My sister's call caught me armor down, in a messy heap on the floor, wondering aloud how this could be the "life at the top" of which so many people dream. Worrying about losing my own health and sanity, and for what? I spilled the story of the nightmare as proof that I was losing my goddamn mind. *In vino veritas*, baby. I swore her to the same bond of secrecy that protected the truth about how my car really ended up in a lake when I was sixteen.

After that conversation, I started journaling everything I could remember about the nightmare each time it robbed me of precious sleep. I was desperate to crack the code and move on with my life already. *Hey, I'm a master problem solver—it's what I get paid ridiculous sums of money to do all day; how hard can this be?* my stubborn head would say to my weary heart at 2:00 A.M.

It was like being forced to watch the same movie again and again—until I finally accepted that pain is a holy messenger. It's going to gut punch you over and over again—through illness, tragedy, nightmares, you name it—until you finally listen.

Anyone else had to learn that one the hard way?

A couple of months later, I found myself starting to practice simple meditation in an effort to combat work stress and Dr. Bob's diagnosis of "monkey brain." Dr. Bob, perpetually clad in a bow tie, tortoiseshell glasses, and jovial mood, was in charge of the executive physical plan to which Harley-Davidson sent its senior leaders for a half-day comprehensive checkup each year. It was a highly respected and well-intentioned program that, ironically, helped us all better understand the myriad ways our jobs (and Wisconsin cheese curds) might be killing us. In my case, almost twenty pounds packed on in the first three years, a grossly-underreported-yet-still-red-flagworthy wine habit, and a brain perpetually stuck in sixth gear. At Dr. Bob's suggestion, I read *Breakfast with Buddha* and committed to twenty minutes of meditation every morning before jumping into a relentless twelve- to fourteen-hour workday. Not exactly getting to the root of the problem. But, baby steps.

One particular morning, I was counting my breaths, allowing thoughts to pass like clouds in the sky, releasing any control or judgment or attachment. Occasionally, my as-yet-unenlightened mind would get distracted by images of Andy, the sexy British voice guiding me on the Headspace meditation app. (Please tell me I'm not the only one!) So, the usual drill. Until I became aware of a new and repeating pattern of thoughts:

Acknowledge me. Listen to me. Nurture me. Love me.

I noticed them and let them pass, as I was taught. But they reappeared, in a hypnotic and rhythmic pattern that I began to chant aloud like a powerful mantra:

"Acknowledge me. Listen to me. Nurture me. Love me.
"Acknowledge me. Listen to me. Nurture me. Love me."

You know that feeling when you just can't shake the significance of something? That twinge in your gut that says, "Listen up, this shit is important!" even though it makes about as much sense to you as ancient hieroglyphics in the moment? That's exactly how it felt. So, I sat for another half hour in complete stillness, perhaps for the first time ever, silently asking the Universe for a little translation assistance.

She delivered, in her own inimitable way. The memory still gives me goose bumps.

On the backs of my shuttered eyelids, I saw an adorable image of a healthy Moka running free in his favorite neighborhood dog park.

As quickly as I felt tears of happy relief welling up, the image of Moka dissolved into a more joyful and carefree *me*—at eleven years old. Me with my sister, in the unfinished basement of our family home on Bass Lake, roller-skating with reckless abandon to the Bee Gees' "Stayin' Alive" and Olivia Newton-John's "Xanadu" on vinyl. The me that played more, laughed more, imagined more, sang more, danced more, loved more, followed her spirit more—and worried a hell of a lot less.

H-O-L-Y S-H-I-T.

This was me before my personality overrode my soul; before I got separated from who I really am and so cleverly donned the rebel alter ego to ward off my deep-seated fears of being disliked, unworthy, or simply a failure. It was the me before I made a career out of looking like I had it all together on the outside while struggle and strife consumed me on the inside. Me before I started should-ing all over myself with the hopes, dreams, and expectations of my parents, employers, society, and men. All the things that had me flexing my identity like a professional contortionist.

It was like a two-by-four to the solar plexus—Moka was my soul.

This whole time, I'd been turning a blind eye to my own neglect of myself, and the Universe was showing me this in the form of the little creature I'd loved most of all. My soul was crying out for *me* to get back in alignment with *me*; back in relationship with my soul— and to trust it to guide me toward purpose and fulfillment, toward ease and grace. So long as I acknowledged it, listened to it, nurtured it, and loved it. Unconditionally.

Loving my soul *is* loving myself. The room inside the room in the nightmare was painful proof of how closed off my way of being had become; of how many layers of armor I'd unwittingly created in an effort to cope; of how distant and disconnected I'd become from my true self.

I sat there for a while, stunned. Trying to make sense of a dizzying array of questions that felt terrifying and out of my depth and like the most important work I had to do in this lifetime:

Have I already sold my soul to the devil? If so, is there a buyback program?

How do I go about reconnecting with my soul? Is it like writing a letter to a childhood friend with whom I've lost touch, and apologizing for being a complete and utter asshole these past few decades?

If my soul hasn't written me out of her will already, how do I go about nurturing her? What does that even look like? What does she need?

Does listening to her mean I have to do what she says? What if she tells me to quit my job and follow my dreams?

Can I be successful and aligned with my authentic self? Are those things mutually exclusive?

Who the hell am I if not the bold, irreverent corporate executive who constantly flipped the bird to tradition?

I knew I couldn't process this all on my own. I needed support. It was time to call on two of my lifelines—my financial advisor and my executive coach. Both already knew I was questioning my future; the restlessness had been increasing for a few years, but I hadn't yet shared the depth and urgency of my struggle. Perhaps I was afraid that if I spoke the truth out loud I would actually have to do something about it. I'd have to be willing to get out of my own way and make significant changes. The kind of changes that require the trust of a trapeze artist as she releases one swing and awaits the next, gracefully suspended in midair.

Dominick, my brilliant but verbose financial advisor, responded with uncharacteristic brevity: "I've been waiting for this call. I didn't think you'd make it past two years at Harley." Phone drop. His instincts were always sharp—in fact, they had helped me to establish what we lovingly (and frankly) referred to as my "Fuck You Fund," a special investment account set up shortly after my eight-and-a-half-year marriage came to a brutal and financially devastating end. It was intended as both a present-tense Fuck You to my ex-husband and a future-tense Fuck You to anything less than total fulfillment in my life.

According to Dominick, my Fuck You Fund was in great shape, after nearly six years of post-recession growth and careful cultivation. I was in no way financially independent, nor was I even close to retirement potential, but I had a little runway to play with if I was willing to bet on, and invest in, the possibility of my future self. If I was courageous enough to step off the corporate Tilt-A-Whirl in order to get serious about understanding my soul and its deepest desires. I just had to get clear on my priorities (and stop buying expensive shoes with red soles).

At the same time, my coach, Victoria, was supporting me in a radical mind-set shift. She understood the profound calling of the nightmare. Despite being funded by Harley, she was dedicated to objectively guiding me through the challenging work of defining what I really wanted my daily life to be like; who I wanted to be in the world; and what values and boundaries I was no longer willing to sacrifice. I bawled my eyes out in nearly every session. I was physically and emotionally exhausted, yet I found perverse comfort in dancing with the leather-clad devil I knew. As much as I dreamt of freedom, I was terrified of being on my own, without the safety net of a big company for the first time. I was the so-called rebel afraid of making the ultimate rebel move. Go figure.

But it was time to reckon with those fears being kicked up like blinding clouds of dust in the wake of the nightmare or the Universe was going to continue to hold me hostage night after sleepless night.

As Anaïs Nin wrote way more eloquently than I ever could, "the day came when the risk to remain tight in the bud was more painful than the risk it took to blossom." I walked out of the corporate world and into my Soulbbatical six months later. And never had the neglect nightmare again. This is the story of risking to blossom.

2.

IF NOT NOW, THEN WHEN?

O f course, the blossoming didn't magically happen overnight. And it didn't come without poignant (if not painful) lessons along the way.

Ten months into my Soulbbatical, just as things were starting to crystallize, my world was rocked by one of those calls that you hope you'll never receive. "Hi, honey," came the soothing voice of my ever-stoic mom. "I don't want you to be concerned, but I'm calling to let you know that Dad had a severe brain hemorrhage this morning. We're at the hospital. He's being rushed into emergency brain surgery."

Welcome to the Paxton family. *Doctors are cracking Dad's skull open to stop massive bleeding in his brain, but nothing to worry about!* We Paxtons always look like we have our shit together. Models of strength. Life of the party. Of course, we're also the collapse-behind-closed-doors-and-cry-silently-so-no-one-can-hear-you types, but we don't talk about that.

I forgot all my "training" with this news and fell into a sobbing heap on the kitchen floor, clinging to my phone as though it were a personal flotation device. For a split second, I wondered if this was another neglect nightmare rearing its ugly head. But my mom's sobering responses made it clear that this was, in fact, our new brutal reality. The lifeblood of our family, my dad, with his fierce intellect, wicked wit, and signature laugh, had been silenced and was fighting for his life.

The doctors weren't optimistic, but my mom was unwavering. Or if she wasn't, she never let on, sitting in the hospital waiting room in Minneapolis for several hours, determined she'd be reunited with her love of the past fifty-eight years. Mom calmly shared updates as my sister and I scrambled to make travel plans from Chicago and Detroit.

I threw a bunch of clothes into a suitcase with record speed. I was on autopilot until I saw a little black dress out of the corner of my bleary eyes, like a dagger of mortality piercing the numbness of the moment. *Holy shit, should I be packing for a funeral?* I don't know if it was denial or intuition, but I did not pack the dress.

When I jumped into my car that afternoon, I had no idea that I would be gone for over a month, or that I was about to get served a master class in life. The true meaning of Soulbbatical was about to be revealed to me. And boy, had the Universe gotten my attention.

Dad survived surgery, but remained in critical condition. I was wholly unprepared for the scene in the neurological ICU the next morning. Maybe some of you can relate. Dad had been fit, tan, and tucking into his ritual dry martini after eighteen holes of golf when I'd seen him last. He'd been teasing me relentlessly for just barely making it home from New Zealand in time to spend Easter with them in Florida. The truth is, I nearly hadn't, almost opting to put off my visit, thinking, *There's always Thanksgiving or next Easter.* But there isn't always anything beyond today. I understood that now.

Three short months and zero warning signs later, there he was lying in the ICU, sedated, pale as the sheets, and connected to countless lines and tubes and machines, all humming, whirring, and beeping in concert to keep him alive. His chest rose and fell in forced rhythm as the ventilator attempted to remind his lungs of their life's work. The left side of his typically perfectly coiffed head of hair was shaved clean, host to a gnarly track of staples holding together the eight-inch incision that gave his swollen brain the relief it so desperately needed. He had aged twenty years in twenty hours. And, as far as I could tell, he was alive only in the most clinical sense of the word.

WTF, Universe? How is this even possible? Mike Paxton is the strongest, healthiest, and most resilient human I know. He never gets sick. He exercises every single day. He doesn't take any medication. He eats like a bird. He can kick my ass running and, honestly, in just about anything physical and intellectual. He aces the New York Times *crossword puzzle every weekend and finishes seven-hundred-page historical biographies in the time it takes most of us to read a magazine. He's the poster boy for "Seventy is the new fifty." Hell, he's too stubborn and driven to go down. So what gives? Is our time here that fragile and tenuous? You can do everything right and still draw the freaking short straw of life?*

I stood in shock at the foot of his bed, overwhelmed by heartache and fear. Strike that. It wasn't fear—it was pure, unadulterated terror. The terror of facing a reality I had never once considered in forty-seven years: life without my dad. Or either of my parents, for that matter. I clung to my mom like a toddler, shaking silently and muffling my heaving sobs in the ample softness of her chest. I wondered if he could hear me somewhere in the depths of a medically induced sleep. Could he detect the suppressed sounds of his eldest daughter, who followed in his executive footsteps to become the CMO of Harley-Davidson, traveled the world on her own, and rebelled against his rules, struggling to find the strength and courage he had instilled in her? Even in that moment, I was afraid of letting him down.

My sister, Christy, arrived the following day, and the three of us sat vigil by his bedside for nearly two weeks, playing tunes by his favorite artists—Bruce Springsteen, Paul Simon, Brandi Carlile, Fleetwood Mac—as loud as we could get away with in the ICU. We relived Mike Paxton's Greatest Hits: memories of late-night family fun after a few too many cocktails, and practical jokes he loved to play on us. He lived to laugh and make others laugh. His signature snort-howl belly laugh was hilarious in and of itself, and wildly contagious. It could be felt and heard for miles, rippling in the hearts of the people we now wanted him to remember to live for.

I held his hand one morning and retold him a story from the summer when I was sixteen years old, and working at Dairy Queen/ Mister Donut (yep, ice cream and donuts under one roof—total teenage dream job, right?). He knew I was working the drive-thru on a busy Saturday night, under the close supervision of Catherine, our tyrannical manager. (Straight-up Beulah Balbricker from the 1980s sex-romp flick *Porky's*. Google her if you're too young to know what I'm talking about or if you're just looking for a good chuckle.) Dad had a plan. About midway through my shift, with epic lines inside and out and Catherine barking orders at the crew to speed up our delivery time, I took a seemingly innocent order through the intercom: "Two Butterfinger Blizzards and a Peanut Buster Parfait, please." I called out the order amid the chaos. Catherine was on top of me in the tiny annex space, designed for one average-sized human to serve customers through the drive-thru window. Then the next car pulled up. It was my dad—with a $20 bill and a shit-eating grin.

"Hey, Shel! How's it going? We've been waiting out here forever." Of course he intentionally screamed it loud enough to get Catherine's attention. I rolled my eyes and grabbed the bill. Well, half the bill to be exact. My dad had pre-torn the $20 so it ripped effortlessly in front of my manic boss during rush hour. For a second, he acted shocked and horrified—just long enough for Catherine to yank me out of the window so she could preempt what clearly looked to be a customer crisis in the making. As she launched into an apology on my sloppy behalf, my dad exploded into laughter and fessed up to his diabolical scheme. We could almost hear him howling the entire way home.

"Remember that, Dad? You were so damn proud of yourself," I whispered as I squeezed all my love and life into his left hand.

And then I felt it. A gentle squeeze in response. The first sign that he really *was* alive. Somewhere deep inside he could hear us and feel us.

I had always hated the Dairy Queen story, until that moment.

Quality of Life

As Dad began to emerge from the fog of trauma, still unable to breathe on his own after nine days, doctors somberly assessed the full impact of the stroke. Extensive tests revealed that his entire right side was paralyzed from top to toes. At seventy-one years old, the former fit-as-a-fiddle-running-twenty-miles-a-week-at-a-sub-eight-minute-per-mile-pace-on-zero-medication CEO would likely have to learn to swallow, eat, walk, talk, write, and read again. *If* he pulled through.

The doctors began to prepare us for the worst. The daily updates were so depressing that we nicknamed the head doctor in the neuro ICU Dr. Dismal. And we found ourselves thrust into sobering conversations about diminished quality of life, living wills, and advance directives. They all felt premature and inappropriate and absolutely maddening. Like the doctors were ready to give up on the guy who was destined to outlive us all. We insisted that they didn't know Mike Paxton like we did. He wasn't even two years into retirement. There was no way in hell he was giving up!

But, I secretly started to worry. Did the doctors understand something that we couldn't yet grasp or accept? What if he really was fully incapacitated? What if he could never golf or run or fish with his grandchildren again? What if he couldn't travel with the love of his life? What if he lost his independence entirely? What if his golden years of retirement became a prison sentence inside his own body? He would be adamant about not living that way. I knew that in his mind, Mike Paxton was nothing if not the patriarch and provider of the family. In his presence, for better or worse, there was never a question of who was in charge. He wouldn't want it any other way.

I wondered where the fine line was between fighting for someone and letting him go. Where did being supportive end and being selfish begin? Could we really even understand what quality of life might mean to someone else? It was so damn subjective.

Since I couldn't crawl inside his head, I dwelled too long in mine, reflecting on my own mortality and expectations. Life suddenly seemed so much shorter. Like, immediately-purge-anything-and-anyone-in-your-life-that-doesn't-bring-you-joy kind of shorter. Don't-ever-say-maybe-tomorrow kind of finite. The idea of retirement struck me as such a senseless concept. Why do we postpone the life we really want until after we're done doing the thing we didn't really enjoy for the best years of our lives? Why wait? What's it all worth if you're not doing what you love every single day? If you're not in alignment with your soul's purpose? Who wants to get to their final moment only to be haunted by the demons of "if only" and "I wish"?

Fuck that. I knew I wanted to go out making a big fat ruckus in this world. I wanted to create my own vision of success and fulfillment before it was too late. Hell, I wanted more than fulfillment. I wanted *soul*-fillment—the kind of inner peace and joy and contentment that permeates every cell in your body. Then I could get hit by a bus or attacked by my own brain or just keel over after mindblowing sex with Idris Elba. With no regrets whatsoever.

I wasn't the only one ready to make a ruckus. Dad began to fight his way back to consciousness after a couple of weeks. That simple hand squeeze soon gave way to the power of breath. He got off the ventilator. His heart and lungs began to carry the torches of recovery. We sat nearby, hopeful his brain would follow.

For the next three months, he validated every bold claim we had made to the doctors. And he lived up to his stubborn reputation. He ripped feeding tubes out of his nose, tried to roll himself out of bed several times a week, and generally got restless with being cooped up inside. At one point, he was forced to sleep in what looked like a jumbo version of a fully enclosed Pack 'n Play for toddlers. He might not have had many words, but his personality and spirit were back in spades.

He graduated from the ICU to the neurology unit and then to three different rehabilitation centers as his condition improved. On the roller coaster of recovery, you could say that we were on the steep and steady initial climb. Not entirely sure what lay ahead, but the anticipation and excitement were building. His right leg started to move ever so slightly. His ability to swallow returned. He was his overachieving self in physical and occupational therapy. He found the miracle of words through classic songs like "Take Me Out to the Ball Game" and "Home on the Range." And he even pretended to read the *Wall Street Journal* with a cup of coffee every morning. Just like the good old days in the corner office.

He was fighting for his own freedom and health and happiness. It wasn't lost on me that I had just spent ten months doing the same thing on Soulbbatical.

Knock, Knock, It's the Universe Again

Recovery is a bitch of a roller coaster. By early October we believed the worst was behind us and set our sights on getting Dad to their winter home in Naples, Florida, before Thanksgiving.

Unfortunately, Dad's brain must have snoozed through that family meeting. It decided to rain on our homecoming parade, in the form of a new brain bleed, this time on the opposite side, unrelated to the initial bleed. It was significantly smaller in size, but enough to cause severe confusion, garbled speech, lack of engagement, and the inability to execute even simple commands. He refused therapy, food, and human engagement, clear signs that he was in trouble again.

Dad's own brain was attacking his former progress. The events of that day were like watching a movie of his ninety-day painstaking progress on 4x rewind, with no pause or stop button. We were heartbroken, and felt so helpless. Just forty-eight hours prior, he had been on a treadmill, supported by a harness, feeling the experience of walking on his own for the first time in months. Yet here we were taking him back to the ER, after the rehab center care team did a preliminary examination and found blood clots in both legs. Fate landed us back in the neuro ICU in the *exact* same room where he'd started this arduous journey ninety-two days before, with the *exact* same Dr. Dismal we loved to hate.

Together, we faced the cruel irony of having survived the "big one," only to be held hostage by the "little one." The first stroke, so massive the doctors gave Dad little chance for survival, met the fighter in him and begged for mercy. His spirit was intact despite the physical and cognitive challenges. The second stroke, smaller and supposedly in a quieter part of the brain, was quite unlike its predecessor, wielding the most devastating damage. It robbed Dad of his personality, emotions, spirit, and his appetite for life (let alone food). He remained in a confused, distant, and tortured state. He stopped smiling and laughing, and spoke barely above a whisper. He refused even the most indulgent foods he used to love. Mike Paxton not lighting up at the prospect of homemade pumpkin pie and Häagen-Dazs vanilla ice cream is a tragedy in its own right.

While Dad would say very little, he did consistently whisper to us, "Something is wrong," his desperate attempt to articulate that his spirit was being held captive. He knew he wasn't himself, yet couldn't access a lifeline, and he was struggling to find hope without it. It was a painful, potent reminder to me that the true essence of being alive is our soul, our spirit. Even when our physical being is compromised, the endurance of our spirit promises love, connection, character, friendship, hope, and the strength to see every challenge as a beautiful opportunity. .

But there wasn't much poetry this time. Our world was Crazy Town, not some bubbly Rosé version of it. In the week after the second stroke, the crazy quotient went up a level when my mom had a scare that landed her in the ER for a day, the flu knocked out my sister, and I tried to laugh through the madness of it all, sitting beside Dad's bed, crafting daily updates for friends and family on CaringBridge and Facebook. This one captures the heartache, the hope, and the hilarity all at once (because that's the way we roll).

Day 96: Mom's up, Christy's down, and Dad is still horizontal.

This chapter feels like human Whac-A-Mole with stress as the relentlessly persistent mallet, attempting to crush our signature strength and resilience. We keep reminding ourselves that the prize is family and future, not an overstuffed plush panda made in China. Most definitely worth the struggle.

Mom is fully charged and back in fine Florence Nightingale form. Christy, on the other hand, is down for the count with a severe cold and ear infection. We've got her quarantined in one of the basement bedrooms with antibiotics, Kleenex, water, and chicken noodle soup, hoping for a speedy recovery, and minimal contagion. Just to be safe, I think Mom and I should dial up our wine intake for a few days. Alcohol kills germs, right?!

As for Dad, it's been five days since the most recent round with his brain. We're seeing the fighter slowly pick himself up off the mat. According to his neurologist, a smaller bleed doesn't necessarily equate to a quicker recovery. In fact, suffering two strokes in quick succession, as Dad did, is quite rare. And can be as devastating as a novice jumping into the ring with Floyd Mayweather. Guaranteed TKO. (Well, the doc didn't exactly leap to heavyweight fighting metaphors but I'm sure he would appreciate my attempt to turn his laborious med speak into somewhat entertaining prose.)

The docs are confident that the bleed has stopped and will be absorbed by his brain over time. No need for brain surgery (which is even riskier the second time around). We're seeing daily "progress" that supports this. I use quotations because progress in this case means painfully retracing the steps of recovery. Re-reawakening his brain to the arts of talking, walking, and eating. As much as we're all reeling from daily déjà vu, the muscle memory seems to be returning. He now just needs more strength to play it out.

Dad is more alert in the morning, but fades pretty dramatically as the sun travels west. No doubt he's still weak, but his vitals are good, his limited speech is returning, and his brain has cued the loop of questions it had on repeat before last Thursday. ("What day is it? When are we going home? How long will we be in Naples? Will we live in a house there? For how long? When are we going home? . . .") Absolutely maddening if it wasn't such a positive sign that the synapses are firing again. I guess we're all learning a little patience on this marathon of a journey.

The highlight of the day was a second video swallow study. (Seriously, it's like the Olympic Trials of the speech therapy world and more exciting than watching him drool apple juice.) Dad aced it and graduated to regular food, with a few exceptions. Most excitingly, he can *finally* drink thin liquids. One step closer to a martini! This is a huge victory because Dad's last hurdle for discharge is to prove that he can eat and drink enough on his own to survive outside of the hospital. His current appetite would starve a mouse.

Dad is generally one of those people in the "eat to live" versus "live to eat" camp. He can run miles on an empty *stomach and not eat for hours afterward. He can survive on a bowl of cereal, a yogurt, and some cheese and crackers for dinner. The Paxton ladies have discussed in earnest the potential of "lifesaving" fat transfers in order to beef up his now waifish 126-pound frame, and to reduce our growing heft. C'mon science, throw us a bone!*

Anyway, we're hoping that recognizable food (not pureed puke on a plate) will help him in the quest for calories. The indulgence of regular coffee alone (versus the chemistry class sludge he's been served for the past couple of months) should have him dancing the jig tomorrow morning! Fingers crossed that his appetite also feels the beat.

Thank you to everyone for continuing to send love, light, prayers, and good juju. We feel it all.

A few days later, Dad was back in the rehab center, but his appetite and spirit were still MIA. It was time for drastic measures. A second permanent feeding tube was surgically reinserted into his stomach. We hoped with every molecule of our beings that consistent nutrition and hydration—and weaning him off some tricky meds—would begin to bring him back. Boost his energy. Help him see the light. And free his spirit from the dark clutches of his brain.

Operation Naples

Come hell or high water, we were transporting Dad to Naples before Thanksgiving. The rehabilitation center didn't think he was ready for release, but we knew he would perish if he stayed. So we got the neurologist's approval to fly, and planned a "jailbreak."

I moved down to Florida to prep their home for his arrival.

There wasn't a question in my mind that I would stay through the end of the year or longer, if needed, and I was keenly aware of the divine timing of all of this happening while I was on Soulbbatical. I wondered what I would have done if I had still been working. I can't imagine for a second not having been there for both my mom and dad during that initial six months. I guess the Universe would have made the decision for me, as she so often does.

We got Dad down to Naples and immediately started to see the restorative powers of his happy place, as well as sunshine, home-cooked meals, and, well, home. My senses of wonder and appreciation were sharpened as I experienced the world through my dad's new eyes, on (st)rolls along neighborhood paths we'd both run many times before, often lost in music or thought. But it was different now, better even. We moved slowly and freely. We lived in the moment. We stopped to appreciate flowers, trees, colors, and the perfect breeze. We participated in the world around us, attempting to assign language and trigger memory. We smiled and said out loud how good it felt to be alive.

But it was far from all sunshine and roses. It's been two and a half years now since that first stroke, and my dad still struggles to unlock the vault of vocabulary to which he once had unlimited access. He can't yet read or write or move his right arm. His OCD, never more than mild before, is off the charts. In an attempt to pick up every leaf from the pool deck, he has driven his wheelchair into the pool on more than one occasion. His temper flares uncontrollably. At least once a week he "fires" one of his caregivers and "divorces" my mom. And he's cognizant enough to understand the gap between what he used to be able to do and what he can do now. He asks the same heartbreaking question on repeat, "When will I be normal again?"

I've never liked the word "normal." I've never known what the benchmark is for normal in any aspect of life, maybe because I've never aspired to it. It sounds boring, easy, and ordinary, not challenging, inspiring, or extraordinary. What's there to want about being normal?

We remind Dad that his comeback story puts normal to shame. He beat the odds. He flipped the bird to the Grim Reaper. Twice. He talks nonstop, connecting the pathways to more words every day, says our names again, and can scream "Goddammit" at us when he gets frustrated. He's back on the golf course, sinking thirty-foot putts as a lefty. His wit is sharp. His spirit is bursting. His laugh is almost at full sonic boom again. And, he's *walking* with a cane. The first time he walked on his own two feet into the country club ballroom, the entire place erupted. Over a hundred people rose to their feet to honor him with a standing ovation that lasted a full ten minutes, until he arrived at his seat. Dad beamed with pride the whole way. Put that in your pipe and smoke it, Dr. Dismal.

We all take so much for granted every single day, obsessing about what others are doing, what we can or can't do, what we think we're supposed to be doing, instead of just being the absolute best at who we are. Thank you for the beautiful reminder, Dad.

This time together made me realize how much I had taken my parents for granted. I recalled a poignant conversation in London a few years earlier when I was with my best friends Sevgi, Markus, and Didem for the holidays. We were sitting around the dining room table of an Airbnb flat having our usual wine-fueled soul talk. I started complaining about the intense pressure I was feeling from my dad—pressure to stay in the corporate world, to push beyond CMO, to make a play for president/CEO of Harley-Davidson, to share his passion for all things business. I think I even said that I wished he'd leave me alone forever so I could do what I really wanted to do. You could hear a pin drop. Sevgi slipped quietly out of the room. An emotional Markus looked me square in the eyes and said, "I would give anything to feel that kind of pressure from my dad again. At least it would mean he's alive."

They each had lost their fathers too soon, and there I was bitching and moaning that mine wanted to see me rise. And was alive to watch it happen.

The Business of Living

Despite the frustrating struggle to find words that had once tripped off his tongue so effortlessly, my dad and I spent endless hours "talking," sitting in the sunshine by the pool, watching golfers on the eighth green behind their home. One day, he gripped my hand tightly, and with tears in his eyes confessed that he had been ready to let go after the second stroke. He'd lived a very rich and accomplished life as a father, husband, leader, friend, golfer, runner, reader, mentor, and martini master, he reasoned. The strokes had robbed him of so much of what he considered his identity, the person he loved to be in the world. It was his time to surrender, he thought. This was when he'd stopped engaging with us and quit eating, the long days when we pleaded with him to fight. I didn't know how aware he'd been of what happened, how close he was to dying (again), and there he was telling me that he'd made the *choice* to live. "I realized I'm not ready to die. I have more work left to do in this life. Different work this time."

Mike Paxton had rocketed from humble beginnings in Hamilton, Ohio, the eldest son of a modest shoe store owner, to become a highly respected CEO and chairman of major companies, and beloved leader and mentor to many. He had given his life to his career, with zero regrets. But now, given the chance to make an even bigger impact outside of the corporate world, he stepped up to the challenge. Whatever that looked like. Sitting there that day, hand in hand, we came to the emotional conclusion that we had both spent our entire lives living business. It was now time to get on with *the business of living*.

Mic drop.

I knew then that my Soulbbatical wasn't coming to an end at the close of that year, or any other. It was just beginning. Soulbbatical was maturing from a personal soul-searching journey into a conscious way of living and being in the world—a commitment to being in alignment with my authentic self and to doing the difficult inner work in order to raise my energy and consciousness and impact. Shifting from a mind-set of surviving to one of thriving.

It was also evolving into my mission, my identity: to inspire others to live their most authentic, courageous, and impactful lives now. Because if not now, then when?

Soul Search
Fulfillment

I have a confession to make. This probably won't surprise you coming from a rebel soul, but I used to be one of those people who frequently skipped over the workbook parts of any book (or anything, really). I was always in a hurry to consume the information and not as eager (or maybe willing) to reflect on what insights were surfacing for me, or to integrate them into my life. My rebellion was to pretend to be "too cool" or "too busy" to do the work. How clever, right? No wonder it took me twenty years to connect with my soul.

When I did start facing those soul-searching insights, though, my world began to change. Dramatically.

These "Soul Search" reflection questions are an invitation to carve out soul time with yourself, to get curious, and to mine your own journey (and stories) for clarity on your beliefs, emotions, intentions, and possibilities. Some of the questions will most definitely make you squirm—and that's a good thing. Trust me. They're not meant to confirm your existing beliefs; rather, they're designed to stir up what's deep inside you. So, stick with it, even when you want to scream, "Fuck you, Shelley!" at the top of your lungs. On the other side of that discomfort is fresh perspective, insight into who you really are and what you really want, and freedom from the old stories and shoulds that are keeping you trapped. I just bared my soul to you— and the rest of the world—so I *know* you're courageous enough to do the same with yourself.

How and when you work through the questions is entirely up to you. This is a choose-your-own-adventure, remember? You can pause at the end of each section to answer the questions or circle back after finishing the book. All I ask is that you spend time with them. And listen deeply.

As Byron Katie says, "Don't believe everything you think." Explore what you want to make true (and untrue)—not twenty years from now but right now.

P.S.: I would love to hear your story. Shoot me a note at shelley @soulbbatical.com and share your biggest insights, inspirations, or breakthroughs from the book. (*After* you do the reflections, rebel!)

S.O.U.L. Process

One more thing before we jump into the first set of questions: I've also developed a framework to help you move forward with any new truth that emerges from the work you do. The goal is to shift from realization to belief to intentional action as quickly as possible. This helps to create new neural pathways in your brain that recognize and support that new truth (and can begin to override the old soundtrack). Trust me—with commitment and practice, it's doable.

So, after answering each set of questions, come back to this framework with one thing (and then another, and another) that blew your mind. That insight that made you say "Holy shit" out loud, or, better yet, that possibility that generated a zing/tingle/radiant warmth so deep in your body that you had to pause and close your eyes for a minute. And then, however terrifying, follow the S.O.U.L. process below to begin putting it into action.

Use this for as many insights as you want. Lather, rinse, repeat.

S: **Show up.** Commit to having integrity with yourself. Stop hiding and playing safe. State aloud the new truth you want to create in service of your authentic self. (It often starts with "I am_____," "I will_____," or "I can_____.")

O: **Own it.** Repeat the truth again and again until you believe it's possible, and then accept responsibility for making it happen. Evict any competing stories and disempowering language (I can't/I should/I have to) from your mind.

U: **Unleash it.** Put clear intentions into the Universe. Share your truth with those who will support, inspire, and/or mentor you. Take one small step toward what you want to create, and witness the synchronicity that follows. The Universe opens one door at a time.

L: **Live it.** Create boundaries and make conscious choices in service of your new truth. Prioritize it. Get creative. Ditch the excuses. Live the idea of who you want to become, or what you want to create, *before you're ready.*

Questions

1. On a scale from 1 to 10, how fulfilling is your life right now?

   1 = My life resembles a dial tone
   10 = I'm dancing like Tom Cruise in *Risky Business.*

   1 2 3 4 5 6 7 8 9 10

   • What would a 10 look like for you?

2. Which parts of your life today make you feel the most alive? Which leave you feeling empty, like you're dying a little on the inside, and consumed with a sense of dread? (Think about work, intimate relationships, family, friends/social life, health and wellness, finances, spirituality, etc.)

3. What are you postponing in life that really matters to you? Where do you catch yourself saying "I'll be happy when . . ."? Call yourself out on this soul sabotage.
   - Why?
   - What's true in that?
   - What's really standing in your way?

4. How are you defining success—on your terms, or someone else's? What does it look like on your terms alone?

5. What are you pretending not to know? (For example, until the nightmare, I was pretending not to know how unhealthy and unfulfilled I felt in my corporate career because I felt guilty for making it to the top and wondering "Is this all there is?" I was attempting to numb my feelings.) Acknowledging the truth is a powerful first step. Be gentle with yourself; sit with what surfaces and feel the emotion of knowing without the pressure to act. Then follow your intuition.

Section 2:

3.

THAT TIME MY CAR ENDED UP IN A LAKE

O nly in an emergency do you think, *I really should've paid more attention to that special investigative report on the evening news.*

Of course, this was back when the news broadcast was a household staple for most of us, before the interwebs were a thing and when only the cool kids got to watch that upstart station called MTV.

What did that guy say to do if you're trapped in a submerged car? Oh, right, roll down the windows as fast as possible and get the hell out.

These were the thoughts racing through my brain as I watched murky lake water seep into the car. I screamed for my boyfriend, Kyle, and his friend in the front seat to crank down their windows. The impact of the nosedive had stunned us all, but no one was visibly hurt. I knew we needed to abandon the proverbial sinking ship before our luck turned (or the powers that be decided our sorry souls were not worth saving).

Kyle and I had been dating for about six months. He wasn't exactly the love of my life; far from it, in fact. He was what I would call a "statement boyfriend"—the statement being me giving the one-finger salute to my parents and their suburban sensibilities. #Priorities. He was nineteen to my not-so-sweet sixteen, smoked a pack a day, worked odd, often clandestine jobs, and lived in his mom's basement decades before an entire generation made that a quasi-acceptable thing. Kyle made my parents squirm all the way through my senior year of high school.

We locked bloodshot eyes in the sinking car, nodded in panicked unison, and took a collective deep breath in. It was Go Time. Of course, the manual window cranks were as stubborn as everything else in my 1978 Buick LeSabre (fondly nicknamed the Spuick for the spray of rust that accented her copper-toned side panels). She was neither built for speed nor a Houdini-inspired water escape. We muscled those windows down with pure adrenaline as the water pushed into the cigarette-pocked suede interior.

I wriggled my way out of the rear driver's-side window with some contraband safely tucked into the front pocket of my ripped jean shorts. I'd only thought to grab the "evidence" seconds before abandoning ship. It was a little late in the game, but I felt a growing sense of responsibility as I watched Kyle and Tim swim to shore. Better late than never, right?

The situation was bad, but it could have been a whole lot worse. We could have plowed through a crowd of young families. The lake was only about six feet deep where the car went in, and the weather had been so stormy that day that the typically busy water playground was a ghost town. I sprinted the twenty-five yards to shore, passing the boys with ease. Who knew that years of competitive swimming would come in handy for an underwater breakout from my own car, driven into a lake by my ne'er-do-well boyfriend? Oh, how the mighty had fallen in two short years. Soaked, standing onshore, the three of us stared incredulously as the roof of the Spuick disappeared.

The events leading up to that moment seemed to have unfolded in slow motion. But it might just have been that my memory was creatively enhanced by the marijuana we brought along on our rainy summer afternoon joyride. (Between us chickens, my money is on the latter.)

One minute we were belting out Pink Floyd's "Comfortably Numb," passing my trusty carved wooden one-hitter among the three of us, and the next thing I knew we were flying high. It wasn't the I'm-so-stoned-life-is-fucking-amazing kind of high; it was more like the wheels-off-the-pavement, *Smokey and the Bandit* kind of airborne, as Kyle lost control of the car. In an instant, our rusted two-tone ton of steel was torpedoing off the pavement and down a steep, tree-lined embankment.

And I watched it all happen—correction, *enabled* it all to happen—from the back seat of my own car. I willingly relinquished control of the wheel to Kyle that afternoon, reasoning (and I use that term very loosely) that he was the more experienced driver (both in general, *and* under the influence). Oh, didn't I mention that I had only officially gotten my driver's license three weeks before? Right.

I sensed the Universe at her mighty pulpit, in that moment, preaching responsibility. It didn't matter that I wasn't the one driving the car, or that I wasn't the owner of the drugs now stuffed in my front pocket, sagging beneath the jagged denim cuff of my shorts. I would need to own responsibility for the very adult situation we found ourselves in.

I handled it about as well as you might imagine. If the Universe was handing out grades, I suspect I'd get a B for ownership, an F for integrity, and an Oscar nod for best dramatic performance by a newcomer.

Here is the short(ish) version. We scrambled from the shoreline to a point midway up the embankment, and quickly agreed on what seemed like an inconspicuous spot to bury the drugs. In hushed silence, we dug a hole with our hands, laid the pipe and pot to rest in the mud, and did our best to re-create Mother Nature's camouflage. Part one of Operation Cover-Up, complete.

Part two was a little trickier. We needed a believable story about how we ended up in the lake, one that painted me in the driver's seat and the motley crew of us as victims of a freak accident. Our budding criminal minds were angling for optimal sympathy and minimal questioning from the police. We already had two "truths" working in our favor: an inexperienced driver at the scene and the hazard of wet roads from the rain. So, what could have driven us off the road so abruptly out here in the wooded western 'burbs of Minneapolis?

Eager to redeem himself, Kyle jumped in first with, "Another car came around the curve, ran us off the road, and fled the scene!"

"Seriously, Sherlock?" I spit back with an eye roll. "Way too complicated. That scenario invites too many questions about a car and driver that don't even exist; too many details to get caught up in or forget. Besides, we haven't seen a single car in the last fifteen minutes. We're out in the sticks. It's us and the deer, and even the deer are smart enough to be hiding in this rain."

Dramatic pause.

"A deer!" the three of us shouted in unison. From sarcasm to epiphany—go figure. I took a shot at stringing it all together. "Okay, so we were on our way to see an afternoon matinee. We were running late so I was driving a little faster than I should have been, especially in the rain. I'll say that part a little sheepishly so I'm admitting to sort of screwing up without inviting too much suspicion. I can even apologize for speeding. Yeah, that's good. Then I came around the turn and out of nowhere a deer darted into the road. I swerved to avoid it, lost control of the car, and skidded off the road into the lake."

"Where did the deer go?" asked Tim, suddenly jumping into the mix to presumably role-play our soon-to-be interrogators.

"How the hell am I supposed to know? Where does a fake deer crossing a real road in front of a bunch of stoned idiots *go*?!" I yelled. "Shit. Wait. Sorry." I apologized after a moment. "That's actually a good question. Was the deer running toward the lake or away from the lake? That's an important detail."

By this point in the conversation, we had covered our tracks after ditching the evidence, washed ourselves off in the lake, and climbed back up to the main road. Back to the scene of the crime.

I looked around with a rapidly sobering set of eyes and imagined myself accelerating around the curve that was now to my left as I stood facing the road. If I was *supposedly* driving the car and *supposedly* speeding and *supposedly* swerving to the right in order to *supposedly* avoid hitting a deer, where would the deer have come from? My brain was starting to hurt.

"The deer darted out from up there!" I shouted with conviction, pointing to the thick woods on the other side of the road. "She was crossing to the lake for some water or maybe she was in search of her lost Bambi and that's why she was in such a hurry to cross. Yeah, that sounds good. She darted out from the left, I swerved right to avoid her, and the car flew off the road and into the lake."

And that, ladies and gentlemen, was the birth of my storytelling career. I'm not proud of the many laws that were broken that day, but I am eternally grateful that no humans or fictional animals were harmed. Of course, we weren't out of the woods just yet. We still had to convince the police.

I rehearsed my dramatic story roadside in the rain, as Kyle and Tim walked in opposite directions in search of help. It turns out that there was a house about a quarter of a mile away, set back from the road. Kyle found the owner home, explained the situation as if it had just happened minutes earlier, and asked him to call 911.

An emergency car-in-the-lake call apparently got designated as a code-holy-shit, automatically dispatching multiple police cars, a fire truck, and an ambulance. My debut performance would have a sizeable audience. Police cars bookended and blocked off the winding road. The paramedics did rapid triage on each of us before confirming that we appeared to be fine. They were incredulous that we didn't have a single bump or bruise among the three of us. The Spuick and her mighty mass had saved our lives. (We hadn't yet seen the brutal beating she took on our behalf.) And then the police moved in. They put the three of us in the back seat of one of the patrol cars like proper criminals. We repeated our fabricated story with conviction in between rounds of good cop/bad cop questioning, and we were offered red licorice Twizzlers from the front seat through the steel grid. We declined, just in case it was a test to see whether we had a case of the munchies. In the end, they had no way to disprove the deer story. It was just crazy enough to be true. And none of the local deer population could be summoned to present an alibi. Phew.

After two hours of questioning and report filing, we were exhausted and painfully sober. And free to go. In a trifecta of teenage luck, we had miraculously evaded injury, arrest, *and* public humiliation.

Of course, this was all before my parents got involved. (Yeah, you were probably wondering where they were during all the excitement. For better or worse, in California on a business trip.)

Keep in mind that this went down in 1986, the dark ages BC (Before Cellular)—though a mobile phone wouldn't likely have survived the swim to shore—so I had no way to call home from the scene. Not that I was anxious to share the news. Interestingly, the police didn't try to reach my parents either. By today's standards, that seems strange, but I was plenty relieved to face the music by myself.

The police unceremoniously dropped us off at Kyle's place, where no one was home. Hours later, following the requisite post-high nap, guilt began to creep in. I knew I should call home before dark. My younger sister, Christy, and I were in the care of an older couple named Margarite and Floyd for the week. (Seriously, you can't make this shit up.)

I suspect we were at the top of a local babysitter blacklist, so my parents had offered top dollar for friends of friends of friends whom we barely knew to squat at our house. Their primary purpose was to ensure that a rowdy party didn't erupt in my parents' absence. I guess no one accounted for the moveable feast that is a delinquent teenager, fresh off a disciplinary year at boarding school, with a new driver's license, a car, and a dime bag of pot.

Oh yeah, boarding school. Just when you thought the story couldn't get any more intriguing, right? I'm telling you: I was *bad* (like, capital B bad) before I was *badass*. My mom still keeps a box of files on all the shit I did to get kicked out of the house at fifteen years old and shipped off to a boarding school to shape up. You know, stuff like getting carted home by the police for underage drinking (on more than one occasion), getting caught storing pot and cigarettes in my bedroom side table (on more than one occasion), and getting into epic battles with my mom that escalated into chasing each other around the kitchen with knives (on more than one occasion). Not exactly the wholesome laugh track material of *Happy Days* and *Family Ties*. Mom's prayer when I was growing up was "Please, God, let me channel this child to adulthood and let us both be alive when she gets there." #Truth.

I know the mention of boarding school sounds privileged and snooty—fair enough—but I feel compelled to tell you that I didn't get sent to one of those prestigious, old money, Ivy League feeder schools on the East Coast. My rebellious ass landed somewhere a little rougher around the edges: a former girls Catholic school merged with a former boys military school to form a sort of unholy union in rural southern Minnesota. I called it "Nuns with Guns."

Little did my parents know that they had landed me squarely with my people. My posse at this school was like the island of misfit toys—the unrated version where the misfit toys have sex and money and raging drug habits. We pooled our weekly allowances (capped at $10 in those days) to buy drugs from the townies at the local pool hall every Friday night. We spent endless hours tripping merrily on 'shrooms and gathering for warmth around our three-foot bong named Lisa (after the hottest girl in school, of course) in a cave down by the river. We skipped classes, jumped out of windows, and routinely snuck off campus. Shattuck-St. Mary's was a rebel's playground, not exactly the iron fist of discipline my parents had imagined.

I was on the dean's list, but not the one your parents brag about to their friends. A rebel in her prime.

So that's a glimpse of what Margarite and Floyd were up against. They couldn't have been surprised when they finally heard about the car. But, of course, it wasn't directly from me. I phoned home, broke the news to my little sister, and left her holding the bag—again. (At the time of this writing, I'm pretty sure Christy still hasn't forgiven me.)

My dad barked long-distance orders to have the waterlogged Spuick towed from the lake, taken to a local auto body shop, and promptly refurbished. The old girl was given a new heart (engine) and a refurbished soul (interior), but he requested that as much as possible of the now even rustier exterior be left as a visible and humiliating reminder of my misadventure.

This car would be my cross to bear, my scarlet letter. Why would my parents ground me, or confine me to the house, when they could delight in my teenage embarrassment at driving a junkyard rust bucket to my first day at a new high school? The Spuick fully embraced her second chance at life, chugging on for another seven years, much to my sister's chagrin. The family laid her to rest sometime in late 1993, long after I had fled home to start the next chapter of my rebel life.

4.

ADULTING AND OXYMORONS

''ve been soul-searching my entire adult life. Trying to make sense of forever feeling like the black sheep in a picture-perfect nuclear family, painfully aware of an alien sensation, like I might be from a different world altogether, wondering who and where my people were and when I might find them. I just kept searching.

I suppose I thought that when I found them, I would find myself. Unfortunately, it took years, though not for lack of trying.

Long after we drove the car into the lake, I pushed to my rebel edges. But years of strict parental and private school discipline had made those edges softer, rounder, duller. Enough that my square peg could finally shimmy into a round hole with little effort. I soon learned that sculpting my identity to meet the expectations of others was a superpower that could open doors, and this new identity took on a life of her own, like an angel overriding my devil tendencies.

Her incessant "why" questions went straight to the heart of who I thought I was.

Why would you want to become a loser like Kyle?

Why not just do what you have to and get out of Minneapolis and your parents' house?

Why not play the game awhile now (and rewrite the rules later)?

I started calling her my "Why-dentity." As you'll see, her armored cape became both a savior and a burden.

I managed to get my shit together enough to graduate with decent grades from one of the best private high schools in the Twin Cities. My parents actually let me come back home for junior and senior year, but there was a deal on table: private school or nothin'. The rebel in me was ready to hit the high road with a kerchief and hobo stick, but my Why-dentity stepped in, convincing me to see it through. It's the *right* thing to do, Why-dentity declared. I'm pretty sure that was one of those trippy *Sliding Doors* moments where a single decision, in a single moment, determines your fate. After all, I could have become a statistic in a tragic headline instead of the author of this incredible story.

Naturally, this early success put my Why-dentity on a bit of a power trip. She stepped up, all high and mighty, to influence the college decision. The definitive plan was to get the hell out of Dodge, that much we agreed on. I was also anxious to escape the conservative, homogenous towns of suburban Minneapolis in search of urbanity and culture and diversity.

So, my proud, self-proclaimed "recovering Catholic" ass rocked up to Saint Mary's College in the fall of 1988. I'm not even kidding. It's like I slipped into a coma during the application process and woke up in a dorm room in Notre Dame, Indiana, surrounded by thousands of perky Irish girls fresh off the Catholic Express. Half were named Molly, the other half Mary Margaret or Margaret Mary or other names with some Virgin-inspired twist. And many were straight up in attendance for their MRS degree. (I never did ask exactly how the final exam was administered for that one.)

I honestly can't explain it. Clearly, I was too stoned to have learned my lesson at the *first* St. Mary's. I'd visited Saint Mary's at Notre Dame with my mom the year prior, and I vaguely remember feeling nauseated by the reigning religions of Catholicism and Football, neither a particular passion of mine. But I thought I might be able to stomach it for the academic reputation of Notre Dame, especially in business. I had let my Why-dentity take this flexing thing a little too far.

Three months later I started College Search Part Deux. I stuck it out at Saint Mary's for the remainder of the academic year, getting serious about my grades while dreaming about a fresh start outside of the Midwest. I don't think the lads and lasses in Notre Dame were surprised (or sorry) to see me go. And neither were my parents.

It would be so easy to blame this colossal fuckup on them. To say that it had something to do with my oppressive Catholic upbringing. To say that my mom and dad insisted on a religion-infused college education since their pious dollars were paying for all of it. To say that they made the decision as karmic payback for the car in the lake, and the cops, and the many sleepless nights I'd given them. But, not a word of that would be true.

My parents were supportive and encouraging in spite of it all. More than anything, they wanted to see me harness my fire to succeed in the world.

The truth is, I was scared shitless of the many questions staring me down at the crossroads of adolescence and adulthood: Who am I? What do I stand for? Who do I want to become? Can I be both a rebel and a success? What do people like me do in the world? I had staked my young identity on rebelling *against* my upbringing, but I was a lost soul when it came to rebelling *for* my future.

At an early age, I started defaulting to what I thought I *should* be doing. I did whatever would satisfy my Why-dentity until I could figure shit out for real. This would be my modus operandi of the rest of my life, and the impetus for Soulbbatical nearly thirty years later.

But I'm getting ahead of myself.

We're still in 1988, and I've just announced a do-over on the whole college thing. This time I was committed to staying awake for it. (In biz speak we would call it "actively engaged," but I wasn't that smart yet.)

In my renewed enthusiasm, I agreed to indulge my dad in the quintessential father-daughter New England college tour, visiting prestigious schools that he never had access to as a first-generation college student from a tiny blue-collar town outside Cincinnati, Ohio. These were schools that he knew would instantly set me on a more fortunate path. Ones that would open doors to the life and career he imagined for me, following in his executive footsteps. They were also schools that I would not likely get accepted to with a transcript that, despite good grades and smarter-than-your-average-bear standardized test scores, read like a cautionary after-school special.

But we dared to dream together, even if only for a long weekend. We took the father-daughter road trip through the stunning countryside of Massachusetts and New Hampshire, breathed in the rarefied air of campuses like Dartmouth, Smith, Amherst, and Tufts, and spent the evenings laughing and sharing our (hilariously different) perspectives on each experience. Dad already had me cast as the editor of the school newspaper and president of the student council. I just wanted to find boys who defied the uniform of polo shirts and backward baseball caps. *Did I walk into a J.Crew catalog?* I mused to myself.

Joking aside, we were bonding in a way that we never had before. I was seeing, perhaps for the first time, a father who wanted the best for his daughter. In that moment, I wanted to make my dad proud. This man, who came from next to nothing, was working his ass off and investing everything in my sister and me. He wanted our lives to be easier than his. And, so far, I hadn't shown much gratitude for it.

As my Why-dentity quipped to me on the flight home from Boston, *Why wouldn't you at least try to make your dad happy? What's the worst that could happen?*

Everything shifted.

I doubled down on schoolwork and the transfer application process. Somewhat miraculously, that effort landed me at Boston College, where I graduated with honors. From the Carroll School of Management, of course.

I still laugh at the fact that the school is affiliated with the Jesuits and had a significant Irish Catholic student population just like Notre Dame, but at least it had the diversity and culture of Boston and the hundreds of other universities surrounding it, I told myself. To be honest, it didn't really matter. It felt liberating to be away from the Midwest, immersing myself in the East Coast vibe and urban life for the first time. I lived off campus, in the hub of Cleveland Circle, in a proper city apartment. And I made new friends from places like New York and California and Europe—all places I had long dreamt of visiting, and maybe even living one day.

I hadn't really been anywhere at that point. Our longest family road trip (in the glory days of the Spuick) had been from Minneapolis to South Dakota to see the famed Mount Rushmore. It involved days of driving, loads of fighting, more Pringles and canned spreadable ham than any human should legally be allowed to consume, and my sister puking her guts out in the back seat. It was so miserable that my dad cut the holiday short and turned around to drive home three days early. It's no wonder we never made it to the coasts, much less beyond.

But I never lost my craving for more distant shores. I was obsessed with maps and atlases and reading about different cultures that I hoped might somehow feel familiar, or reveal something profound to me. I dreamt of having my own passport to magically transport me to the exotic lands my pointer finger would discover at the spin of the globe in my dad's home office. Australia, South Africa, France, Brazil, Mexico, China, Iceland, and all those magical little islands scattered like pebbles across the mass of blue oceans. I wondered who lived in those faraway places. And who was lucky enough to *visit* them.

Boston might not qualify as exotic, but she was the first siren to call forth my innate wanderlust. Her history blew my mind, and her intellectual and creative energy were like rocket fuel. I was bursting at the seams. I wanted more. I knew I had to find a way to see the world.

At some point I started to see a career as my potential round-the-world ticket. Maybe my dad *was* onto something.

The summers after my sophomore and junior years in college, I landed internships at big-name advertising agencies in Chicago. I'll admit that, from day one, I was completely dazzled by the swank offices, stylish people, sexy travel, and iconic client brands. These were the fat and happy days of full-service advertising—yes, my young friends, once upon a time creative, media, account services, research, strategy, and production all lived under one glorious high-margin roof—and I was hooked. This seemed like a pretty kick-ass way to make a living until I figured out what I really wanted to be when I grew up.

Just before graduation, I found myself in the plum position of having two job offers in hand—one in NYC and one in Chicago. The job market was bullish in those days, and I had stepped up my game pretty significantly. I wanted to be an account executive at one of the premier global ad agencies, come hell or high water. I also flirted with a well-known consumer packaged goods company, which would have put me on the traditional brand-management path, but I lost out to someone with an MBA. Knowing what I know now about that world, and me, I suspect that was divine intervention. Thank you, Universe.

Despite the gravitational pull of NYC, I decided to return to Chicago to start my career with one of the biggest and best advertising agencies at the time. I had fallen madly in love with the Windy City during my summer internships—the lake, the architecture, the arts, the diversity, and the cultural buzz, all fed my soul. And the top-tier agency not only offered to put me into an accelerated leadership development program in client services, they were going to start me out on an iconic brand: Wheaties. The Breakfast of Champions. I felt like a freaking rock star. And I got to shoot TV commercials with Michael Jordan! (The basketball legend. The OG before there was ever a Michael B. Jordan.)

I don't hail from a lineage of doctors or lawyers. Far from it. I'm more closely related to the likes of Speedy Alka Seltzer, the

Pillsbury Doughboy, and the Jolly Green Giant. Remember those guys? They're all part of the many brand stories that my dad had a huge hand in shaping while on his corporate rise. Marketing runs deep in my veins. My attraction was preordained. But as I look back, it was perhaps a little too easy for the black sheep with a rebel soul and infinite curiosity. Had I settled for someone else's dream at the expense of defining my own?

I didn't have time to think too hard on it at first, working my butt off days and nights and oh-so-many weekends. The recognition and perks fueled me when I had nothing left in the tank. I was quickly promoted from the farm team to the big leagues. Two years in, I was asked to work on McDonald's, one of the largest accounts at the agency. I know, I know. Not necessarily one of the healthiest brands but a juggernaut in the marketing arena. A great place to hone my skills. I'm ashamed to admit it, but I was so eager for the account that I hid the fact that I was a vegetarian (for years). Even worse, I convinced myself that it was okay to compromise my values for validation. They wanted *me*.

There I was traveling to L.A. for shoots, staying at Shutters on the Beach in Santa Monica (an oceanfront boutique hotel I still can't afford on my own dime), and flying to London to meet with Disney executives on the *101 Dalmatians* movie set (not to mention being put up in a suite at the Dorchester, one of the ritziest hotels in London—and that's a high bar). I finally had a passport, and had crossed the Atlantic for the first time! This career thing was paying off. Well, for my Why-dentity at least.

The ad business had become my whole world. A few years in, I sensed my own life and priorities starting to reflect the shallowness and demands of the business. My life had become a one-legged stool, albeit a brilliantly shellacked one.

My roommate at the time was a dear friend and work colleague (of course) named Laura. She and I used to joke that we'd get paid more per hour working as Starbucks baristas (yes, we did the math) and our souls would be dancing because we'd actually have time to read and go to movies and date and do more of the things we love. This conversation happened pretty much every weekday morning at 5:55 A.M., in the entryway of our local Starbucks, as we were the first people in line for coffee before jumping in a taxi to head to the office. We would rarely get home before 8:00 P.M.

Like all good humor, there was a kernel of truth. The rebel was getting restless again.

I'm not about to go all righteous or spoiled bratty on you. I didn't take my career for granted for a single second. I knew how fortunate I was to have the kind of opportunity and exposure I was getting at such a young age. I was living a real-world MBA. In fact, humility and gratitude are what made it difficult for me to think about blazing new trails for so long. How could I leave this career, and thumb my nose at the luxury of private school and a debt-free four-year college education? My parents had worked so hard to set me up for traditional success. How could I disappoint them? And, how could I not do everything in my power to become a role model and mentor for other women in business?

Still, I felt a growing sense that I was meant to be doing something else. Something unexpected. Something courageous. Something that would satisfy my deeper, edgier desires.

So, I took up improv comedy as a side hustle, for creative nourishment. I was in Chicago, after all, home of The Second City, which introduced Bill Murray, Steve Martin, Dan Aykroyd, John Belushi, John Candy, Steve Carell, Tina Fey, Amy Poehler, and so many other comedy legends to the world. Tina and Amy were not yet the household names that they are today, but they were rising stars on the local scene. I knew of Amy because we went to Boston College at the same time. We didn't know each other (sadly) but I was a huge fan of her work in My Mother's Fleabag, the campus improv comedy troupe. She kept me laughing through the collegiate angst of exams and boys and epic weight gain. (Thank you, Amy!)

I like to believe that I've lived a life without regrets, but that isn't entirely true. There are a few that you'll learn about as we get to know each other better. The first two were big misses in college: not doing a semester abroad and not scratching my itch to be onstage. I justified staying in Boston junior year because I had transferred in as a sophomore and was looking for continuity after moving around like someone in the witness protection program since the early high school days. But the reason I didn't audition for improv was deeply rooted in fear and shame. I was funny—everyone told me so—but I had gained a lot of weight since swapping the life of a competitive swimmer for a competitive drinker. I was terrified of being the funny fat girl whom everyone laughed at for all the wrong reasons. I couldn't even get a boyfriend, for fuck's sake. (Not since the glory days of Kyle, anyway.) Why would anyone want to watch me jiggle around onstage? So I chose to keep hiding.

Until about a year into my advertising career, when I felt that itch again and finally decided to take my own bull(shit) by the horns. Some of it had to do with the fact that I spent the first year after college getting healthy and shedding the weight. I gave up meat and took up running. (Or as close as I could ever get to running with the equivalent of two bowling balls strapped to my chest.) I was starting to feel better about myself, inside and out.

The rest of showing up for improv had to do with the provocative "I'll-do-it-if-you-do-it" challenge of a close friend and work colleague. Mark-Hans and I were kindred rebel souls, yearning for more depth and meaning and adventure beyond advertising. (Not coincidentally, it was he who would recruit me into Harley-Davidson many years later.) And we were just brave and crazy and funny enough to cannonball into the comedy deep-end together.

We spent the next nine months of evenings and weekends training at the Players Workshop of the Second City before cofounding our own troupe, the Oxymorons. We performed a combination of live improv and long-form comedy sketches on a tiny community stage in Lincoln Park every Saturday night. We were in our element, writing and performing edgy material inspired by the cultural zeitgeist of the early '90s—from Somalia to the Clintons. We were living in the moment and tapping deep into our creative souls. It felt so energizing. And liberating. And terrifying.

As much as I loved improv, I wasn't quit-your-day-job-on-the-road-to-SNL good. Living up to our name, we were at best a partial success. But I did learn some invaluable lessons:

I was never going to be Tina or Amy. It was time to own being Shelley.

Fear never completely releases you from its clutches, no matter how seasoned you get. The goal is to learn to dance with it, transforming it from nervous resistance into energetic momentum. It's funny how long it took me to translate this from the professional stage to my personal life.

Improv is the best training for life and business. It's grounded in the principles of agreement and collaboration and momentum and opportunity. It's all about working together to build bridges and advance a story. "Yes, and . . ." is the pivotal phrase in improv—it moves a scene forward. It's also one of the most powerful phrases in our language. Honestly, I attribute most of my business success to what I learned at the Second City. (No doubt I improvised my way through many a boardroom.)

Feeling energized and terrified is *always* a sign that you're pushing your edges and growing and exactly where you are meant to be. Lean into whatever it is that makes you feel that way. You'll be astounded by the opportunities it creates.

Case in point: Mark-Hans pulled me aside one Saturday night after a performance of our comedic spoof on *Grease*—featuring Bill and Hillary Clinton as Danny and Sandy (it was 1994, after all)—to share that he was planning an epic five-month journey across Africa. His vision was to start in London, England, and finish in Dar es Salaam, Tanzania, tackling Mount Kilimanjaro and a whole lot of the developing world along the way. And he was walking into the office that Monday morning to request a leave of absence.

My jaw dropped, and I swear I felt my soul scream.

"Wait a second, you can do that?" I asked, incredulously. It seems my Why-dentity had been at the helm for so long, I'd forgotten how to break the rules (and to ask for what I really wanted).

"I don't know, but I'm sure as hell gonna try," M-H retorted with a natural confidence that I'd come to know and love (and envy, if I'm honest). "And, if they don't want to give me the time off, I think I'm just gonna resign. I have to do this, Shel. I'm young and free and may never get the chance to do something like this again."

It was like the portal to a whole new dimension opened that night. My mind was spinning for the rest of the weekend. I journaled pages and pages of questions. Was my restlessness a calling to go do something life changing? To set off on some bold and ballsy adventure by myself? Where would I want to go? Was Mark-Hans going to pull off this sabbatical thing and open the door for the rest of us? If not, was I brave enough to walk away from my career, even if temporarily, to scratch this itch? And what if it turned out to be more than an itch?

I declared that day that I wanted to backpack solo around Europe for a whole summer. It may not be as exotic as Africa, I reasoned, but my first trip to London had been a teaser to the main course of continental Europe. I was salivating at the thought of being immersed in languages, cultures, histories, cuisines, and landscapes. I'm pretty sure I even drooled on my journal, smudging the starter list of countries I would visit: England, Portugal, Spain, France, Italy, Germany, Austria, the Netherlands, Belgium, the Czech Republic, Poland, Hungary, Croatia, Slovenia . . .

I had felt so much pressure to begin my new career, and to prove to myself that I could do this adulting thing, that I hadn't even entertained the idea of traveling after graduation. I fast-forwarded through the fun, straight into adult life. Let's be honest, the (brilliant) British idea of a gap year of travel between school and work would never have flown through the filters of my Why-dentity at the time. No doubt she would have pushed back with her usual challenges: *Why would you travel when you have this amazing job offer in hand now? Why would you risk not being able to find another job like this one?*

I realize now that I hadn't even stopped to consider my own needs or wants at the time. I naively saw the situation as a false choice between what others expected of me and what I wanted for myself. A few years later, it was time to flip that script and start asking, *Why* not *me? Why* not *take time to explore and see what else is out there beyond advertising and the corporate world? Why* not *travel more while I'm still young and single and relatively free?* The arguments were compelling.

The agency gave Mark-Hans the thumbs-up on taking *five months off* for his trip, but the stipulations were clear: they wouldn't hold his job or guarantee him a job when he returned. But, if there was a job available at his level, he'd be first in line for it (as long as he landed back in Chicago within the five-month window). That sounded like a pretty low-risk/high-reward deal to him (and to me). We were fortunate to have seats at the table of the extravagant feast that was the early 1990s advertising scene. The agency was winning new business hand over fist, and clients were paying top dollar. Chances of no jobs being available were slim, and, let's be honest, neither of us even knew if we would want to return to advertising after flirting with life's infinite possibilities.

I spent every waking moment of the next several months planning my journey and refining my pitch to the powers that be. I didn't want to pounce too quickly after Mark-Hans, but I also didn't want to risk the embers of generosity cooling before I made the request. What was the worst that could happen? My boss could say no, and I would have to decide whether to stay or to go. But I would have done the hard thing of courageously asking for what I wanted. Maybe that's the real lesson I was meant to learn anyway.

I waited until halfway through Mark-Hans's journey to have the conversation. Thankfully, this was before I learned that he went down from heatstroke in Mali and got stranded, incommunicado, for weeks in the wilds of Zaire (now the Democratic Republic of the Congo).

As with most things, the actual conversation with my boss wasn't nearly as scary as the zillion dress rehearsals (and gremlin voices)

in my head. In the moment, my nerves were settled by a glance
out Jim's office window, toward the vastness of Lake Michigan and
the endless horizon of opportunity. I found myself speaking from
my soul, perhaps for the first time in the context of my career. I
revealed my deep yearning to expand my horizons, to welcome the
world as my classroom, to somehow help others along the way. And
I surprised myself by voicing something completely unrehearsed:

"I think I may be testing the waters for an international assignment. I feel like I'm meant to live and work somewhere else. Like I
could be the person that you send to the place in the world no one
else wants to go."

I scared the bejesus out of myself. Was this my Why-dentity
cleverly nudging her way into the conversation? Was she trying to
make it seem like we had a master plan when we were really in
search of so many answers? I knew that I wanted to see the world
but I still had so many questions about my life (im)balance, my career, and my creative passions. But the agency loved the possibility
of grooming another general for the front lines of global expansion.

Boom. Just like that, at twenty-six years old, I was given the
green light for a four-month leave of absence. What I didn't realize
back then is that this would become my very first Soulbbatical.

The typically endless Chicago winter passed quickly as I shifted from planning into execution. This trip was no longer one of the many fantasies scribbled in the hopeful pages of my journal. It was living proof
that I *can* create what I want; that the Universe *does* favor the bold.
I was high on possibility as I finalized my route from Lisbon to London (by way of at least fourteen countries), purchased a Eurail Pass,
pored through Lonely Planet and Berkeley travel guides for the best
youth hostels and "can't miss" experiences, scratched out a rough

shoestring budget, pared down my belongings to the backpack-able bare necessities, and booked stints in two Volunteers for Peace programs, one in the Czech Republic and one in Poland. Nervous energy and adrenaline alone could have rocketed me across the Atlantic. But I bought a plane ticket to Lisbon, just to be safe.

By spring, I was out of my apartment, sleeping on my friend Eric's couch, counting down the days. I said tearful goodbyes and prepared emotionally for the biggest leap of my life (read: drinking my way through the rising terror—perhaps not particularly enlightened, but a good foundation for life in Europe, as it turns out).

Pillow Butt

I hung around just long enough to witness my little sister marry her college sweetheart in Detroit. I served as Christy's maid of honor in a very traditional Catholic Church ceremony, standing beside her on the sacred altar of St. Alphonsus. And by standing beside her I mean sweating like the proverbial (or not) whore in church, fearing that at any moment a single bolt of lightning, headed in my direction, might take the whole place down, incinerating all four hundred of our closest family and friends. As everyone else recited The Lord's Prayer, I prayed for some sort of temporary parochial pardon (hoping there was such a thing). No one was shouting out the Amens more passionately than me.

I love my sister with all my heart and soul. I would have done anything not to ruin her special day (despite the fact that she convinced our parents to replace me with a Shih Tzu puppy the year I got shipped off to boarding school). Thankfully, the worst that happened that day was far from the church.

During the picture-perfect reception dinner at historic Greenfield Village, the rebel in me decided we could all use a little break from the tyranny of tradition. It was time to stir things up. I was the older, not necessarily wiser, unmarried, hell-raising sibling leaving her very respectable job to backpack solo around Europe. My sister might have been following the script, but that certainly didn't mean I had to.

Using the familiar clinking of the champagne glasses to rally the attention of all fifty tables, I stood at the front of the massive hall to offer a somewhat unorthodox toast. I was going full Second City on this crowd.

"Congratulations, Christy and Derek! I love you both so much. You are clearly soul mates who found each other on this crazy journey we call life. It's been fun to witness. As Gene Wilder said in *Willy Wonka & the Chocolate Factory*, one of our favorite childhood movies, "'We are the music-makers, and we are the dreamers of dreams.'" Let's raise our glasses to the music you'll make, the dreams you'll create, and the love you'll celebrate together. Cheers!"

I waited for the applause to die down before continuing, "All righty, then; with that formality out of the way, let's get down to the *really* important stuff. I'd like to take a minute to properly welcome Derek into the Paxton family, to prepare him for deeper integration into our rituals and rites of passage. Derek, now that you're officially on the inside, you've earned the right to understand how we really roll. And, as your new sister-in-law, I want to make this as comfortable as possible for you. I want you to *feel* like a Paxton, like you have what it takes to belong in our family."

I paused to reach under the head table for the props I had stored ahead of time. As I was standing up again, I caught my sister's gaze. Her eyes were already laughing. She knew I was going for it and she was on board. In my hands were a king-sized bed pillow and a brown leather belt.

I stood facing Derek, my back to the room, as I dramatically strapped the pillow across my king-sized ass and belted it firmly in place. Paired with my fitted, floor-length bridesmaid's dress, this was avant-garde fashion at its finest. The look alone provoked hysterical laughter, and even a few wolf whistles, from the crowd. My comedy ego was peacocking. Big-time.

I grabbed the microphone again and began to work the front of the room like a Parisian catwalk.

"You see, Derek, this is how Christy and I grew up. The Paxton household had a lot of rules. I mean, *a lot* of rules. Mom and Dad have relaxed a bit in their old age, but they were crazy strict about everything: chores, homework, curfews, church, TV time, boys, swearing. Especially swearing. I've had more than a few bars of Ivory soap in my dirty little mouth. Funny, it never got any fucking cleaner.

"When we intentionally broke the rules, Christy and I would sprint upstairs to our bedrooms and prepare for the reckoning. Belting huge pillows around our little waists. Mike Paxton may look small, but his spankings are fierce. By the time he was finished with us, we would have full-on baboon butts. Red and swollen and impossible to sit on. This was 1970s-style child-rearing at its finest.

"Pillow Butt eventually became a family joke. It's quite literally the fabric of our story. So we want you to have your own . . . just in case. Welcome to the family, brother."

The crowd was roaring. Christy and Derek were doubled over in tears and laughter. Even my mom was in stitches. But my dad wasn't finding it quite as humorous. In fact, he looked like he might kill me.

You would've thought I had just driven another car into a lake. Good thing I had a flight to catch.

5.

MY FIRST SOULBBATICAL

anding in Lisbon a few days later, alone and overwhelmed, I gave myself a little pep talk in my journal. *I will never regret this trip. I am realizing a dream and taking time to sort out my life and focus on myself. I'm finally relaxing and letting the winds carry my body and soul.*

Letting the winds carry my body and soul. Wow. I'm awestruck reading those words again, over twenty years later. Even back then it seems I had this blossoming sense that if I could just let go of what I thought I *should* be, the Universe would be my gentle guide into what I *could* be. She would become the Sherpa of my soul as I attempted to summit this thing called life.

But the art of letting go is something that would take me decades to learn and master. First I would willingly and repeatedly subject myself to the pain and disappointment and heartbreak of control. Starting with Gabriel.

As the gods of adventure would have it, just three weeks into backpacking I met an amazing man in Córdoba, Spain. Gabriel was a kindred spirit, traveling solo, seeking divine inspiration on his future direction. He was from Portland, Oregon, though I never would have pegged him as a fellow American when I first saw him relaxing in the open courtyard of the stunning Mezquita-Catedral. He was blessed with beautiful olive skin and dark hair, appearing at ease in the intense sun of southern Spain. Like it was his natural habitat. It turns out that he was a unique blend of Filipino and another Southeast Asian island nation, as well as Scotch and Irish. I cracked myself up by wondering if that made him a spicy drunk? I wanted to find out.

What I remember most vividly are those gorgeous brown eyes and massive dimples smiling in my direction. I was taking a break from sightseeing, soaking up the rays in a vain attempt to convert my Midwest winter white into some kind of Mediterranean sun-kissed sexy. I still had a ways to go, but that didn't seem to bother Gabriel.

From ten feet away, he spotted the Berkeley travel guide in my lap and pulled the identical edition out of his backpack with a knowing wink in my direction. This was one of the few benefits of backpacking in the pre-Internet days—you could filter for "your people" by which travel guides(s) they were carrying. Lonely Planet and Berkeley were known for being more adventurous, off the beaten path, and liberal. I had met my match, if I was judging this book by its cover alone.

With a wave of the hand, I invited his dark-and-handsomeness over to the tiled space next to me. We clicked immediately. Bypassing small talk for soul talk in minutes. Drawn deeper by our shared sense of purpose and possibility and chemistry. We quickly discovered that we had both chosen to backpack on our own in order to challenge ourselves, and come to terms with our deepest fears and desires. The Universe was putting at least one of us to the test, as she pulled the strings of serendipity that day.

"What are you doing for the rest of the day?" Gabriel asked with a gaze hotter than the noon sun. "Scratch that—what are you doing for the rest of the month? Let's get lost and found together."

He wasn't joking. He felt it, too.

I was still too stubborn to fully trust the Universe, but I accepted her nudge. Sitting next to me was an irresistible invitation to begin acknowledging my fears and letting them go. To lean into what I came here to do. My fifty-pound pack was heavy enough—it was time to lighten the emotional load.

"Ha! And he's a romantic idealist, to boot!" I shot back playfully and fake-swooned for dramatic effect. "Seriously, I'm flattered. I'm yours for the day. But, be warned that I turn into a pumpkin at midnight. My chariot, in the form of a bullet train to Madrid, leaves at the crack of dawn tomorrow morning."

WTF? I didn't even pause long enough to consider the idea of a spontaneous change of plans, of an unexpected adventure with a sexy and kindred soul for a couple of days. Apparently my hard-charging head still had my tender heart in a stranglehold. I was superwoman on a tight schedule. As if this was another day at the office. [Sigh.] I'd clearly forgotten what I had written days earlier about letting the winds (or a really special guy) carry my body and soul.

"Why are you in such a rush to get to Madrid? You meeting someone there?"

"No. It's a stopover on my way across the country. My mom is meeting me in Barcelona in four days."

I was excited to see my mom, even if it felt a little too soon into the trip. I was just finding my groove, but I loved that she was flying over to show her support. And to spoil me with a luxury hotel escape from the raucous and stark youth hostel scene. I admitted to Gabriel that it had taken me a long time, perhaps too long, to understand and appreciate the importance of family. To realize that their love inspired my confidence. I'm sure they had concerns about me not only leaving a great job, but also trekking across foreign lands by myself. (And making strange bedfellows along the way!) But they never breathed a word.

Our long, lazy lunch turned into a stroll through the palimpsest of religious history that is the historic old town of Córdoba: Moorish towers, Roman bridges, mosques-turned-cathedrals, and the famous Jewish Quarter. While most of the town slipped into the traditional afternoon siesta, we savored every minute of feeling so awake in each other's presence.

We managed to separate ourselves for two hours to "clean up" for a nice dinner together. Back in my room at Pensión El Portillo, I depressingly surveyed the contents of my backpack strewn across the bed. Yikes. What was I thinking when I packed this heaping pile of unsexiness? Where was my full wardrobe when I needed it most? All those stylish dresses and tops and skirts and sandals gathering dust in a storage locker thousands of miles away. A far cry from the only clean items staring up at me now: a white cotton tank top and full-length tie-dye wrap skirt. Paired with black combat boots, I looked better prepared for a Phish concert than a night out in Spain. My fragile self-confidence was plummeting.

"Hey. You look great," Gabriel whispered as I stepped out the front door of the pensión exactly two hours later. (Remember that quaint time before cell phones when everyone used to be on time?) He was there waiting for me, as promised. Hair slicked back in a ponytail. Fresh black T-shirt. Same perfectly worn jeans and boots and dimples.

"You're sweet. Thanks for saying that. I don't know about you, but I'm already regretting some of my packing choices. I'm gonna have an epic bonfire with some of these rags in a few months!" I responded with my usual self-deprecating humor. I still hadn't learned to receive a compliment or to believe in the power of my inner beauty. He laughed and leaned in to kiss my cheek. For a second I wondered what I looked like through his adoring eyes.

The next several hours were a blur of shared tapas and laughter and dreams, and mucho *vino tinto*. We were lost in a world of possibility. As we strolled hand in hand from bar to bar, I felt like I had known this man all my life.

Suddenly the deep and resonant chimes from a nearby cathedral penetrated our private universe. Striking exactly twelve times. It was pumpkin hour, way too soon.

"Are you still hell-bent on getting to Madrid tomorrow morning?" he asked, putting his arms around me and pulling my body tight to his.

I closed my eyes and allowed myself to cocoon in the crevice of his chest and breathe in the memory of this moment. I wasn't ready to respond, or to leave him. He honored my silence by holding me close, gently stroking my hair, and waiting patiently for a single word that was sure to determine our fate.

I don't know how many minutes later I managed to lift my head up and pull just far enough away to connect with Gabriel's soft and hopeful eyes. They were already searching mine for the answer. Pleading with mine to take a chance.

I stood on my tiptoes and touched my lips to his. It was our first kiss. And it was as freaking electric as I had imagined it would be.

The intensity increased as his tongue tried to seduce mine into saying I would stay.

In that moment, I felt so alive and so carefree—and so insanely confused. Did I really want to screw up my plans on a whim? For a guy I just met this morning? Did I want to risk being late to meet my mom? Even if I stayed another day or two, was a fly-by-night romance what I was after on this journey? Was I even ready to get naked with this guy (because that's clearly where this was headed)? My head was pinning my heart to the mat again.

I panicked.

"I'm so sorry, Gabe. I have to go to Madrid. But, I really don't want to say goodbye. Can we please find a way to meet up in a few weeks? Maybe in France since we're both heading in that direction?" I was choking on my own words.

"Yes," he spoke with such quiet confidence. "I don't want to see you go, but we will find a way to meet up." He kissed me again. It felt like a promise. "This has been one of the best days of my life. Thank you for spending it with me. Now let's get you back to your pensión before you really do turn into a pumpkin, Cinderella. I think it's too soon for me to see that." He winked and put a comforting arm around me as we started walking back.

Outside the front door of my place, I pulled out my journal so we could swap addresses and phone numbers and rough travel plans. It was still a few years before the world would be traveling with mobile phones so we committed to leaving each other good old-fashioned landline voice mails. Audio bread crumbs to help us find our way back to each other.

"Good night, Cinderella. I'll see you again very soon." He was a gentleman. He kissed me passionately one last time and walked away.

"Don't forget! I'll be in Paris in a few weeks!" I called out into the night.

My journal entry later that sleepless night says it all: *I just watched him walk away. I'm a fucking idiot.*

Two months and seven countries later, while doing volunteer work in the countryside of the Czech Republic, I called my voice mail to check in. Bookended by messages from friends back home was a voice that still gave me butterflies. It was Gabriel. He said he missed me and wanted to hear my voice. He left the details of his remaining travel plans in hopes that our paths could still cross— maybe in Vienna or London before the end of the summer?

Despite trying for a few more weeks, we never connected or spoke again. I was being called to greater adventures—and heart-break.

I moped through the museums of Madrid in a first-class funk before happily catching a train to Barcelona a couple of days later. My fragile heart was ready for some Mom love—and distraction. It wasn't long before my senses were under the influence of Barcelona's intoxicating tastes and colors and sounds and smells. Barcelona, you vixen. You had me at *hola.*

The next morning I grabbed a *café con leche* and navigated my way from the youth hostel over to the five-star Claris Hotel, steps off the swanky Passeig de Gracia, to wait for my mom, who was on a red-eye from Newark. Me and my human-sized backpack and frayed denim shirt and combat boots would just be chilling in the luxe marble lobby, on a sleek modern couch, facing a gallery wall of rare and perfectly illuminated art and artifacts, making the impeccably tailored staff very nervous. This hotel was clearly more attuned to hosting the invariable dressed-to-the-nines jet set than the intrepid I'm-sweaty-but-I'm-fine pack set. The rebel in me was snickering with every glance, daring the staff to approach me so I could announce that I was, in fact, their guest for the next week.

As I luxuriated in the coolest place I had sat in weeks (literally and figuratively), I was aware of my growing anticipation. I was genuinely excited to experience this beautiful city with my mom. She had loosened up over the years, or maybe I just wore her down with all my high jinks. Either way, we were finally starting to enjoy spending time together as adults. Dare I say we were on the verge of becoming close? This was a dream come true for my mom. She had always longed for the kind of mother-daughter relationship that involved talking every day, sharing intimate details, asking for life advice, and traveling together. All things that triggered my independence and defiance growing up. I had refused to give her what she wanted for all those years, choosing instead to remain distant and detached, letting emotional immaturity limit our potential. Now I could finally see that travel was a brilliant starting point for more authentic and meaningful bonding. I'm forever grateful that she was willing to connect with this wild animal in her natural habitat.

Susan Rae Paxton stepped out of a taxi just after noon, looking surprisingly fresh for having just flown nearly eight hours across the Atlantic. She was a statuesque and striking woman in those days: tall, curvy, legs for miles, thick waves of long dark hair elegantly pulled back at the nape of her neck, and porcelain skin that taunted the intense Spanish sun. She exuded confidence and positivity, and flashed her radiant smile at the bellhops as they eagerly opened the lobby doors. Despite frequent comments about how uncannily alike we look, I never saw myself in her beauty. I was obsessed with the lethargic metabolism and fuller body shape I had inherited—a big chest, a rounder torso, and thin legs sprouting out beneath it all. I dubbed it the "apple on sticks" body type—and I hated it. I hated how soft and feminine and eager to expand it was.

My mom had always been sympathetic to my struggles. She tried her best to buttress my sagging self-confidence and distorted self-image. In her cheerful and inimitable singsong style, she would recite her cheesy-but-poignant "You can do anything" mantra, tailored to the crisis at hand. It went something like this: "Honey, you're smart, you're strong, you're beautiful, you're talented, you're creative, you're funny. You can do anything you put your mind to!" After merciless teasing from my sister and me, and the creation of some pretty clever parodies she still hasn't heard the end of, she switched gears. She engaged in an act of comedic jujitsu that would help pin my demons to the mat. Or at least give me the solid footing to do so on my own.

One day in my mid-teens, at the peak of our push-and-pull, I arrived home to a little gift from my mom. I don't remember the details surrounding the moment, just that it carried the weight and significance of a peace offering. An olive branch in the form of a wooden plaque carved and painted to resemble a very large female sheep. In bold black letters, on a stark white background, it celebrated, "Ewe's Not Fat, Ewe's Fluffy!" Yep. That's exactly what it said. If any of you have ever wondered where my wit and humor come from, look no further than this defining moment. I learned early on that laughter brings strength and sanity and humanity and perspective (and that I might want to look into the benefits of a good shearing).

So, yeah, this is how far we had come. With maturity and experience under my belt, I was able to admit how incredibly lucky I was to have a mom who shared such powerful words and beliefs and unconditional love and support, despite my very conditional response.

I was beginning to see how much more of that we needed in the world, especially we women.

As soon as I saw her, I abandoned my backpack and customary too-cool-for-school rebel saunter and ran to greet her. I have no doubt that this was a surprise for her too. She was used to my aloofness, but never stopped believing that the shell would crack one day. I felt the immense understanding and gratitude in the reciprocity of her hug. We both understood that this was a new beginning.

The next several days were exactly that. Time spent bonding over incredible art and architecture, delicious and exotic food, royal and Olympic history, day-trips to beach towns, picnics in the park, getting lost in the Barrio Gótico, and relaxing at the Claris Hotel's gorgeous rooftop pool with cocktails and books. I was still deep into reading *The Fountainhead* by Ayn Rand. (Yes, I'm exactly the kind of book nerd who chooses to carry a heady 750-page tome as one of her "bare necessities." For the record, Ayn was only a brief rebel obsession.)

Funny enough, the most special memories my mom and I share from that week together were the result of seemingly mundane activities like developing film and doing laundry and reading mail. (In case you needed any reminder that we're still in the mid-'90s, we developed five rolls of camera film so I could share the initial legs of my adventure with my mom. Did I also mention that I was traveling with a Sony Walkman?!)

I'd arrived at this luxury boutique hotel with a backpack full of filthy clothes from a month on the road. My mom politely suggested that we send the majority of them to the hotel laundry service, at her expense. I was still tripping over the shoestrings of a budget mindset. I insisted that we wash my clothes by hand in the deep soaking tub in our bathroom and then hang them to dry like proper Europeans except without windows that open . . . or a drying line . . . or the support of a breeze. A day and a half later, our sleek-if-more-than-a-little-humid duplex room looked more shantytown than Shangri-la with half-dry, half-moldy clothing draped over every fixture, railing, shower rod, and piece of furniture. #budgetfail. The next morning my mom promptly sent every last ratty sock and tank top and pair of underwear to be properly cleaned. When we returned from sightseeing late the following afternoon, we walked in to find the most unexpected and ironic presentation on the bed: each and every piece of cheap clothing pressed, folded, and wrapped individually, like new, and artfully arranged in four matching woven baskets adorned with fresh flowers and a handwritten note. For the low, low price of $500. We laughed for hours and wondered how much cheaper it would have been to just buy new stuff instead. In hindsight, I should've gone for the wardrobe upgrade!

My mom also brought piles of good old-fashioned letters for me from family and friends: my sister, roommate, best friend, improv friends, Great-Grandma Sprandel, Grandma Wiggins, and Grandpa Paxton. Most people had been mailing notes to American Express offices in major cities along my route, but this bundle of love carried by my mom felt extra special, even before I opened the envelope from my grandpa. His was the last in the pile. Inside was a long letter—unusual for a proud man of few words (he was quite happy to leave the storytelling to my boisterous grandma)—and five two-by-three-inch sepia photos of war-ravaged Florence, Italy. Each picture had a cryptic location note in its thick white border, in the same fastidious all-caps handwriting as the letter. Wow, my grandpa took these photos during World War II! I glanced up at my mom to gauge her reaction as I carefully placed each photo on the coffee table in front of us and began to unfold the letter.

"Did you know he was sending photos from his time in the war?" I asked.

"No," she responded with astonishment as she picked up a couple of the photos for a closer look. "I've never even seen these photos, and I'm sure your father hasn't either. Grandpa Paxton doesn't talk about his time in Italy. I only know that he was wounded in combat at Anzio beach. He took shrapnel within inches of his heart, so they sent him to Florence for treatment and recovery before finally sending him to the Cleveland Clinic back home. Doctors were never able to remove the shrapnel because it was too close to his heart to operate. The cruel irony is that it still threatens to kill him to this day."

She paused, registering a combination of sadness and empathy and growing curiosity about the letter in my hands. "Grandpa was deeply scarred by the whole experience. He never wanted to speak a word about it, or travel to Europe again in his lifetime. So, what does his letter say, honey?"

Wow. I hadn't known any of this. Here I was, in Europe, learning a powerful piece of family history that happened fifty-some years earlier and fewer than seven hundred miles down the French and Italian coasts from where we sat in that moment. My journey was creating a kind of multigenerational connection I could have never anticipated. I took a deep breath and started reading.

I wish upon my grandpa's Purple Heart (one of the many incredible things I learned about him that day) that I still had that letter to recite from today. I'm devastated that it got lost in the shuffle of travel and moves and divorce and God-knows-what in the subsequent years.

But a few passages stuck like Velcro to my soul. I remember that he praised me for *my* courage in choosing to make this journcy. He wrote that he envied my desire to see the world (the war had snuffed out his) and wanted me to understand the history of at least one of the countries I was planning to visit. A history shared from the perspective of a twenty-one-year-old US Army infantryman from a tiny town in Ohio, who had never traveled beyond his own state, suddenly fighting the Germans in the Battle of Anzio in Italy. He shared the fear and pain and tragedy of being on the front lines of a brutal stalemate for months. He explained that his pack-and-a-half-a-day smoking habit (now addiction) began as a way to cope with the loss and destruction and hopelessness at times. And he revealed the little he remembered about the fateful day that the Germans took the high ground and opened fire on the Allied troops below. That same day he became one of the statistics of the war—and earned his Purple Heart.

Decades later, while on Soulbbatical, I would serendipitously find myself standing on Anzio beach at the end of a three-week visit to Rome, Florence, and Tuscany. Channeling the strength of my grandpa Paxton as my dad, his eldest son, was fighting another battle altogether.

But, sitting there in Barcelona that day, tears streaming down my cheeks, I felt I had a mission. I wanted to share modern-day Florence with my grandpa. To share images of hope and survival and reconstruction juxtaposed against the devastation he witnessed. To share the results of what he risked his life for. I wanted to thank him for *his* courage, both in the war and in sharing his stories for the first time.

After a week with my mom, and in one place, my stubborn independence and wanderlust were raring to get back on the road. Experiencing Barcelona first class, and having the bonding time with her, was such a treat. But I was champing at the bit to cross new borders, meet new people, and get dirty all over again.

For the next month, I wandered through France, Belgium, the Netherlands, Germany, and Switzerland. I could feel my sense of self deepening and shifting with each new landscape, from the lavender fields of Aix-en-Provence, France, to the majestic mountains of Interlaken, Switzerland. Along the way, I became drug-free (after a horrifying experience involving a laced space cake), I dreamt about performing and touring with Boom Chicago (a Second City improv group that set up shop in Amsterdam), I added Turkey to my "must visit" list (on my growing list of possible trip extensions), and I wrestled with some deeply ingrained aspects of my identity. On the train from Switzerland to Italy I wrote in my journal: *I want to be reasonably uninhibited by the end of this journey. I want to feel free to be and act without the burdensome concern of the judgment of others. I want to feel only the burden of self-knowledge, so that I will no longer be able to ignore or suppress my true passions. Only act on them!* Wow.

I rocked up in Italy bursting at the seams with confidence and anticipation. Not only because Italy was a place I'd always wanted to visit but also because a close friend—who, for the purposes of this story, I'll call Evo—was meeting up with me for this stretch. And we had a beautiful mission: to re-create Grandpa Paxton's World War II photos in Florence. Right after we adventured by train, foot, and bicycle through Milan, the Cinque Terre, and Tuscany. Actually, Tuscany almost ended our friendship when he convinced me to go on a single day, sixty-mile self-guided bicycle tour through (ridiculously hot and hilly) wine country, instead of renting a car like sane people. Forty-odd miles into the ride, at the top of a monstrous hill, I told Evo to fuck off for ruining the romance of this postcard landscape forever. Not one of my finer moments.

Still, we made it to Florence on speaking terms, and immediately threw ourselves into the challenge of re-creating my grandpa's
war photos. Searching for landmarks we could identify in the pictures was a fascinating way to explore a city neither of us had ever
before seen. It felt like our very own postwar *Mission: Impossible*-
meets-scavenger-hunt adventure, clues leading us from the banks
of the Arno to the American embassy to the iconic Duomo and a
historic tower in the now famous Piazza della Signoria, home to the
Uffizi Gallery. We would show the original pictures to locals and
shop owners in an attempt to identify the exact bridges, buildings,
plazas, and angles captured fifty-two years earlier. Our resourcefulness and ambition rewarded us with spot-on re-creations for three
of the five photos over the next couple of days.

The first was taken from just behind a bridge bombed out by
the Germans—the view was looking down the Arno, over the ruins
of another bridge, toward the historic and untouched Ponte Vecchio. All the bridges were completely reconstructed and beautifully
intact in the modern-day photo, and the Ponte Vecchio was crawling
with tourists. The second was a close-up of the actual Brunelleschi-
designed dome of Santa Maria del Fiore with war-torn Florence
as the backdrop. We mimicked the shot from the bell tower of the
cathedral, after climbing 463 very narrow stairs to an open roof
with a jaw-dropping 360-degree view of renaissance and resilience,
not rubble. How the hell my grandpa got up there with shrapnel
threatening his heart, we'll never know. The third sepia photo was
a lone tower, standing guard over a single structure amid the remains of fallen buildings and a single military vehicle. A friend of
the owner of our little pension deduced that it could be the tower
of the Palazzo Vecchio, a fortified fourteenth-century palace. Sure
enough, approaching the palazzo from Via Vacchereccia on the op-

posite side of the Piazza della Signoria was the exact shot. Looking up from the street, now bustling with shoppers, past a row of sturdy ochre buildings with deep green shutters, was the sentry tower still watching over the heart of Tuscany.

That very same night, making our way back to our room after dinner, we wandered through Piazza della Signoria once again. In front of the Palazzo Vecchio was a live opera and symphony performance, beautifully and dramatically choreographed with sound and lights against the centuries-old backdrop. As we sat on the storied steps to take in the show, my mind kept flashing back to my grandpa's photos. What a far cry from how our generation is experiencing Florence (and all of Italy) today. I was suddenly desperate to capture all the beauty—the sights and sounds and feels and life—to share with him. To package it in a magical salve that might begin to heal his wounds. That might help him feel like the fight was worth it.

What I ultimately created from those few days in Florence was a photo collage so he could see modern-day Italy juxtaposed against the devastation he'd witnessed. His worn sepia photos next to my fresh colorful images, framed in gold as a symbol of wisdom and courage and compassion. He apparently cried when he opened it, and then proudly displayed it in his living room as a conversation piece. Sadly, the photos arrived only a handful of months before George Frederick Paxton, Jr. died of late-stage cancer at the age of seventy-four, with the shrapnel and trauma of World War II still enshrouding his heart.

Evo and I parted ways in Venice. He was on his way back to the States and I was headed toward the Czech Republic, where I would begin volunteer work with Volunteers for Peace, a nonprofit organization hosting programs designed to help less fortunate countries and communities around the world. I had signed up for a combination of manual labor and teaching English in rural areas of the Czech Republic and Poland. I felt driven to help the people of these former communist countries accelerate their free-market dreams and upgrade their quality of life. And I was anxious to spend time in less developed places after seeing so much of western Europe. My tolerance for tourists was wearing as thin as the cuffs of my denim shirt.

Eastern Europe had experienced the Velvet Revolution and collapse of the communist regime just seven years earlier. It was also the gateway to Croatia, Slovenia, Romania, Turkey, and so many other off-the-beaten path destinations I was learning about from my adventurous new friends along the way. They told me about opportunities to help war refugees in Croatia and to teach English in Greece and Turkey. Listening to their stories, I expanded the list of countries I wanted to visit to include Greece, Russia, South Africa, India, Vietnam, Thailand, Brazil, and more. I had barely scratched the surface of a single continent.

Before and after volunteer service, I spent extra days steeping myself in the rich cultures of Prague and Kraków, imagining myself as an expat in this part of the world. Suddenly wondering whether the work of my life was travel—or was travel the life of my work? I continued to wrestle with questions about my career on the pages of my journal: *That is still the unsolved mystery—to return or not to return to my career? I truly can't imagine not having a "real job," but then again two years ago I couldn't imagine the reality of traveling through Europe for four months by myself. I think it may be time to face the music of my soul.*

That soul track inspired me to buy travel guides for new countries and to seriously consider extending my journey beyond four months to push farther south and east. It opened my mind to the possibilities of teaching English or finding other paid work along the way. And it encouraged me to dance with the idea that maybe I didn't have to choose between travel and work after all. *Maybe*, I thought, *that's only what I think I should be doing because that's the false choice others are subscribing to.* It was such a liberating thought that I must've subconsciously sent a powerful bat signal to the Universe.

I made my way to Vienna from Budapest, where I had been scrubbed to within an inch of my naked life by some very large and aggressive and dangerously braless Hungarian masseuses in a traditional Turkish bath. (Silly me. The Ottoman Empire was never really known for being gentle or hospitable, now was it? I was already writing the comedy sketch in my head on the train.) Vienna seemed like a good place to check in and recalibrate while eagerly awaiting a new layer of skin. It also happened to be a geographically ideal jumping-off point for whichever direction the winds of my soul would carry me:

> *The west representing the known and more certain path. My final two weeks of the trip journeying toward London and Chicago. Likely returning to the agency.*
> *The south/east representing the wild frontier of an exhilarating but undefined future. Making it up as I go. Taking the rebel road less traveled.*

As if on cue, I received a voice mail upon arrival in Vienna. Sandwiched between the usual fun and supportive messages from friends (most of them getting excited to welcome me back home soon) was one that caught me completely off guard. One that just might have been the Universe responding to my indecision with a swift kick in the ass.

The president of the agency in Chicago wanted to know if I would be interested in running the McDonald's business in Istanbul, Turkey. Holy shit. Whaaaaaaaaaat? Rewind. I replayed the message three times to make sure I had heard it right. Sure enough, not only had the agency won the McDonald's business in Turkey, they clearly remembered my parting words: "Like I could be the person that you send to the place in the world no one else wants to go." Coincidentally, a place that had since made it onto my growing wander-list. The Universe was up to something.

My head was spinning. There was more detail about flying to Istanbul for an interview within the next two weeks, and needing someone in place in Istanbul within six weeks to get the business up and running. Suddenly I was back on business time—everything fast, everything urgent, and everything on their terms. That part made my stomach churn, after months of slowing down and gaining perspective. But there was a part of me that was undeniably intrigued and already laughing hysterically at the thought of traveling to meet a potential new employer, in a predominantly Muslim country, in a sundress and combat boots. #winning.

I found one of Vienna's famous coffeehouses and sat down to pour my thoughts out on the page. To make sense of the shit storm of conflicting emotions. My journal entry from that day says it all: *My immediate reaction [to the Istanbul opportunity] was HELL, YES! My own positive reaction caught me off guard after all the promises I've made and personal goals I've set as a result of this journey. Helping to further the McDonald's monopoly is the antithesis of the creative road I've decided to follow. But I can't resist the prestige and allure of an international job in an exotic location.*

A few days later, still deep in processing mode, I followed that up with an entry that still sends shivers down my spine: *I've made so many promises to myself about improving my quality of life, aligning with my passions, getting back into improv—that'll all be on hold for my career again. How important, really, is my career?*

Apparently important enough to convince the powers that be to let me fly back to Chicago, ditch my pack-rat gear, and dig out some respectable clothes before hopping on a plane to Istanbul, three short weeks later. A global job seemed like a win-win—I could scratch the itch of my wanderlust *and* take my career in a bold and ballsy direction. That was starting to feel on-brand to me. I believed it was the rebel choice, not the false choice. A coloring-outside-of-the-lines dream that combined a respectable job with the nontraditional lifestyle I craved. Maybe this is just the kind of reasonable compromise that adulting requires.

Three months later I found myself extending the lease on my ten-by-ten-foot storage unit in Chicago and saying goodbye to friends and family for the second time in the same year. This time my life whittled down to two massive suitcases, my passport, and a dog-eared copy of *Culture Shock! Turkey.*

I can see so clearly now that I was setting up the perfect system to get what I wanted in ways that didn't require tremendous risk or vulnerability or epic WWE-style battles with my Why-dentity. A system that would serve me for years to come in terms of opportunity and success but would consistently sidestep the real longing of my soul. I think these days it's called a "spiritual bypass."

6.

REBEL HIDE 'N' SEEK

Moving to Istanbul, for me, was a way to satisfy my rebel edge within a respectable business career. To be honest, this flavor of corporate (and living, in general) was becoming another kind of addiction for me. The "seeking" lifestyle capitalized on my innate courage and nomadic instinct. It enabled me to choose mobility over mainstream. It wooed my ego with the sexiness of world travel, iconic global brands, and the career envy of others. Of course, it also kept me distracted from the deeper questions of identity and priorities that I didn't want to face. Perhaps I was addicted not only to seeking but also to hiding.

I was playing my own (precarious) version of Rebel Hide 'n Seek, perpetually feeding my curiosity because I was afraid of what I'd have to see if I sat still with my own needs and desires. Using my wanderlust to avoid coming home to myself. Perhaps I was hiding and seeking so I couldn't actually *find* myself. After all, that was the whole point of the game when we were kids, right?

I left Chicago for Istanbul ecstatic about pioneering new personal and professional frontiers, amid warnings from friends and family not to inspire the sequel to *Midnight Express*, a 1978 film in which a young American gets thrown into Turkish prison for trying to smuggle hash out of the country. If you haven't seen it, let's just say it's not a flattering portrayal of the Turks or their hospitality or their prison system. I'm thrilled to say I avoided discovering how accurate the prison situation in that film might or might not have been. But its larger depiction of Turkey, I can confidently say, was wildly inaccurate. I fell in love with the culture, the food, the history, the language, and the people—one person in particular—Candan, (pronounced John-Don) my future ex-husband. I thought he was my permanent souvenir, but as it turns out, that honor goes to the blue glass "evil eye" that still hangs above my front door in Chicago, to ward off bad luck, and ill will and creepy dudes. (Okay, I might've made up that last one. A girl can dream.)

Candan and I met at the local agency in Istanbul, where we both worked. He ran the largest account at the agency, which also happened to be the biggest bank in Turkey. Happily, beneath the calm, unflappable "account guy" shtick that had his conservative clients eating out of his hand, he was a wildly creative spirit who had studied photography and filmmaking at university, with a minor in marketing. He had stumbled onto the business path when a lucrative media sales gig came his way after graduation. He leapt at it because he was determined not to follow his dad and older brother into the struggling family business—a modest neighborhood market, their family's bread and butter, quite literally, operated beneath their home in Izmir.

Candan was warm, wholehearted, and hardworking, a generous spirit who introduced me to his country, and a belief in soul mates. In Turkish, his name even means "from the soul." I thought it was a sign from the Universe.

Despite feeling a magnetic pull toward something deeper, we remained friends for the first year. I was only supposed to be in Istanbul for a six-month assignment, and falling in love was most definitely not part of my plan. Rather, my experience told me it was more likely a fast track to disaster and heartbreak (and a total buzz-kill on all things rebel).

I blew through that six-month marker, and when the local agency wanted me to continue leading the McDonald's team, plus take on other international brands like Johnson & Johnson and Frito-Lay, I was all in. The brass back in Chicago loved that idea. They'd already concluded that Istanbul would be the perfect hub from which someone could manage and grow the McDonald's business in southern Europe, North and South Africa, the Middle East, and India. Had they been reading the pages of my journal and sent a love note to my soul? I was a "Hell yes, sign me up."

I couldn't believe how much faith agency leadership had in a twenty-seven-year old who was flying by the seat of her pants. But who was I to ask twice? Somewhere along the way I had figured out that courage begets confidence, not the other way around. What I lacked in courage, I compensated for in pure moxie. And by moxie I mean determination, spirit, and a hell of a lot of over-giving: always being available to clients, working late nights and weekends, and loads of travel away from the city and the man I was falling in love with. It was stimulating work, so it felt worthwhile. I didn't see the toll it was taking on me or anyone else. I was hardwired to dig deep, make it up, and offer 100 percent of myself until I had the same level of confidence in me that others did—that is, pretty much for the rest of my career and life.

Honestly, I couldn't have imagined going back to the States after only six months anyway. There was still so much I wanted to see and do. Turkey was expanding my horizons in ways I couldn't have imagined. Istanbul bridges the West and the East, Europe and Asia, but for me it was a gateway to so much more. I was just starting to learn the language; managing like a boss to haggle for figs and spices at the markets and guide a taxi back home without ending up on the Asian side of the Bosporus. But not well enough yet to make my cleaning lady understand that my favorite T-shirts were not to be shredded into rags for washing the floors, and that Brillo Pads weren't the best tools for cleaning freshly painted walls. Hell, I had just discovered that people eat whole fish from the sea and that olives grow on trees. Where I was raised, fish came in sticks, and olives came in glass jars, with little red pimento peppers stuffed inside.

Istanbul felt more like home than anywhere I'd ever lived. If I didn't look like the spitting image of my Irish-English-Scottish-American parents, I would have thought that my mom had had a wild affair with a Turkish student at the University of Cincinnati. (Side note: I was born while my dad was still in business school and my parents lived in a tiny studio in married student housing. According to Paxton family lore, as a baby I slept in a drawer inside a closet. Perhaps that explains everything—my rebel nature, my intense claustrophobia, and my unquenchable desire for freedom.)

The local agency was becoming like family. I was no longer the strange (and only) foreigner occupying one of the many desks along the windows in the open concept office. I had become a respected leader and a trusted friend. Not only had I clicked with Candan, but we had also found the other members of our tribe in kindred spirits named Sevgi and Didem. We were all orphans in Istanbul. Sevgi was born in Turkey, raised in Canada, and had just returned to Istanbul in her late twenties to explore her roots. Didem was the product of an academic family who had lived all over the world. She was born in England and raised in Saudi Arabia and Turkey. Her family was in Ankara, and her advertising career was in Istanbul. Her future husband, Markus, was a Finnish-Canadian living in London and commuting to Istanbul. And, of course, Candan's family was running their business in Izmir, on the Aegean coast. We were like an international version of the Breakfast Club.

Thanks to a private language tutor, I was starting to string together full sentences, learning to express myself beyond "Hi," "Thank you," and "No, I don't want to marry you." I was even beginning to understand the portion of work meetings that inevitably devolved into a passionate debate in Turkish. Turks don't hold back. They're a heart-led culture, committed to feeling and expressing the full range of emotions, from anger to love. They're short on filters and long on forgiveness. They're direct and honest and can hold a stare for an uncomfortably long period of time. No "Minnesota Nice" passive-aggressive bullshit like I grew up with. They say it like it is. I still remember how liberating it felt to work in an environment where courageous conversation prevailed.

Of course, I also remember the first time an agency colleague looked me in the eye and said, "You've gained weight." It stung on impact, but it was the undeniable truth. My love for Turkish food—especially the carb-o-liciousness of börek, gözleme, pide, and baklava—was catching up with me. It was my first clarity around the relationship between authenticity and courage, and the power of speaking the truth versus the drama of dancing around it. I realized then that I would take truth over tap-dancing any day of the week.

But, just in case you're thinking I totally had my shit together, let me assure you that my third-grade Turkish language proficiency also got me into trouble on more than a few occasions. Two examples come to mind immediately—one infinitely more embarrassing than the other so let's ease in, shall we?

Istanbul had the local delivery thing nailed long before the concept of Amazon Prime Now was even a digital embryo. Every local market (and there were tens of thousands of them across the city of eighteen million people) carried all the basic necessities from eggs to laundry detergent to alcohol. You could call down to your local market at nearly any hour and have items dashed to your door by an eager, young sprinter-in-training. It's commonplace in a culture that takes hospitality seriously, but for me it was an invitation to be lazy when I simply didn't feel like walking down the stairs and around the corner. It was also an opportunity to practice my Turkish, with mixed results. Let's just say it wasn't unusual for me to end up with tobacco cigarettes instead of sigara böregi (a savory phyllo and cheese pastry rolled up like a cigarette).

And then there was that Friday night at a club in Etiler. I had woken up that morning with a sore throat, and feeling achy, but decided to push through anyway (as I did in those days) because I wouldn't miss a night out with Sevgi. (Ah, the glory days of FOMO, before I fell madly in love with JOMO.) A few hours in, we were dancing with a group of fun guys who might've been hoping for a little action. One of them leaned in close to me and said in Turkish, "What are you doing after this?" (I think.) I was too weary to string together a proper sentence in Turkish, so I combined exaggerated sign language with English words to respond that I was feeling ill and about to call it a night. I dramatically stroked my throat with my hand, pointed to the exit, and shouted over the music, "I'm sick. I'm feeling very sick. Time to go home."

Before I could repeat the gesture, he planted a big wet kiss on me. This got Sevgi's attention. She knew I only had eyes for one guy, and it wasn't Mr. Hot-and-Horny, now standing inches from my face. After a few minutes of yelling and translating back and forth, Sevgi pulled me off the dance floor to share the horror and hilarity of what had gone down. Apparently the word *sik* in Turkish is slang for penis and, even worse, the throat-stroking gesture means "to give a blow job." I'd unintentionally played the aces of sexual innuendo, and this guy thought he had won the booty-call jackpot.

But a good challenge always revs me up. So I persevered with learning the language and culture, the rebel outsider anxious for an invitation to become an insider. I wanted to be liked. Beneath the rebel armor, I was a purebred people pleaser. Which might explain my decision to start smoking again. Yes, you read that right; and, yes, it's a disturbing statement. It felt like an impossible dilemma at the time: working in an open-plan office in a country where 98 percent of the population (by my guesstimation) chain-smoked. At the best of times, the office looked like a Beyoncé concert, with smoke machines in full sultry effect. At the worst of times, it was San Francisco on a day when you could hardly make out the defining red peak of the Golden Gate Bridge. Either way, I couldn't take it. My eyes watered and my lungs burned. The secondhand smoke was going to kill me one way or another, so why not take matters into my own hands?

I got Sevgi over to my apartment one night with the invitation-slash-warning that she was about to become my smoking coach. She was already a heavy smoker. I, on the other hand, hadn't taken a drag off a cancer stick since my high school days (aka the pot-smoking, car-in-the-lake days). In preparation, I bought a couple of bottles of Doluca, the best of the worst of the Turkish red wines, and a pack of Marlboro Lights. We talked and smoked and drank until I was green and gagging. But I never stopped. I was determined that this was the way to survive in my current environment. Oh, the irony.

Simply put, I was willing to go to incredible lengths to cope with things that were satisfying my ego, but not my soul. What I called "survival" was really about belonging. It felt rebellious, even if I wasn't being true to myself. I despised smoking, even as I was doing it. Only now, thanks to Brené Brown's work, am I crystal clear that belonging is actually rooted in authenticity. As she says in the documentary *The Call to Courage*, "True belonging doesn't require you to *change* who you are; it requires you to *be* who you are." Boom.

But I can't deny that that adventure cemented the beginning of a lifelong friendship, rooted in something much deeper than cigarettes and booze. Sevgi and I became soul sisters. Actually, we became the Sylvesters, a nickname birthed on another hilarious night in Etiler. Leaving a bar, we walked out the front door to find a massive fur ball of a cat perched on the garden wall in front of us. That alone wasn't an uncommon sight; an army of wild cats and dogs roamed the streets of Istanbul. But this cat was a different character entirely. He was a healthy black-and-white tuxedo with a mischievous, almost animated grin. He looked like he was about to tell us a joke or break into song and dance. Sevgi and I glanced at each other and, in perfect unscripted synchronicity, let loose our frighteningly fabulous Sylvester J. Pussycat impersonations, "Shhhhufffering Shucotash! It's Shhhhylveshter!" And that's what we've called each other ever since. Even Didem and Markus's son, Luka, now calls us his aunt Sylvesters. This felt closer to the silly, gut-busting laughter kind of belonging I really wanted in my life.

The Sylvesters, and our little orphan tribe, experienced Istanbul together in its modern cultural heyday. It was the beginning of a vibrant creative renaissance before the earthquake, economic crash, and the extreme politics of Erdoğan. We were working hard and playing hard. There were gorgeous summer nights in open-air restaurants and bars along the Bosporus, and winter nights at music clubs in Etiler and Taksim. We went to parties and industry events. We loved the festivals, especially the Istanbul Biennial that staged modern art in some of the city's most stunning Ottoman treasures. There was a constant sense of discovery and adventure.

And I was a proud ambassador when family and friends came to see who and what was keeping me on the other side of the world for so long. I loved showing off my new home.

Meanwhile, I was still satisfying my rebel by working with clients in Greece, Egypt, South Africa, India, and the Middle East, dropped in there as a kind of agency fixer. It was exhilarating. In between meetings, I fell in love with all things Mediterranean in Greece; discovered warmth and creativity and the game of cricket behind the crime-ridden façade of Johannesburg; got seduced by the beautiful trauma of India; and witnessed the bigger-better-shinier one-upmanship of Dubai.

But it wasn't all unicorns and rainbows. I also saw the darker sides of culture and business. As a single woman without a male companion, I never got to venture deep into the Middle East, even for business purposes. It was my first direct exposure to what it was really like to be a woman in other parts of the world, to be made to feel "less than" my male counterparts.

And a seamier underbelly of business came onto my radar as I was asked to do something (sort of) illegal for the company. No, I wasn't smuggling hash, or any kind of drugs for that matter. I was essentially smuggling myself, in and out of Turkey. Because the company had me on a tourist visa for the first couple of years, I needed to exit every three months in order to stay on the good side of the law (and avoid becoming *Midnight Express II*). Going in and out of the country every three months wasn't technically illegal, but working in the country on a tourist visa certainly was. Border patrol looked closely at reentry dates to catch anyone trying to do exactly what I was doing, and often denied entry if a suspicious pattern was detected. (Like, maybe, doing it eight times over two years.)

So, to avoid scrutiny, and the extensive paperwork of a legal work permit, the local agency would send me off to the airport every three months, with an envelope stuffed with instructions and shit tons of cash. Once there, I was whisked down corridors, behind barricades, into secret rooms, and straight to the gate of my departing airplane, paying off men in dark suits and uniforms as I went, and coming out the other side with the "right" stamps in my passport. All this thanks to the nameless crew I called my "Bribe Tribe." Then I would do it all over again when I returned a few days later.

These quick trips would often land me in Vienna, Austria, where Kevin, one of my bosses, was based. Kevin was a beloved character in the McDonald's world—a life of the party, living-on-the-edge, anything-for-the-client account guy. He lived for work and vodka, not necessarily in that order.

Kevin's drinking could create connection or chaos in an instant. The problem is, you never knew exactly which you were going to get, and I was on the "clean up" end of chaos more times than I'd like to admit. It was part of the job as long as I was willing to tolerate it, or as long as I wanted to succeed in this part of the world.

I started to wonder about the strength of my own boundaries on one particular visit to Cairo, Egypt. The well-connected owner of the local agency had been invited to a party at the US ambassador's residence, and we were his guests. After a couple of cocktails at the bar, a woman approached Kevin and immediately started fawning, "Mr. Belushi, we are so honored to have you with us tonight. We weren't expecting you. Would you be willing to do a few select autographs and photos while you're here? The ambassador's daughter is a huge fan." I forgot to mention that Kevin was a dead ringer for Jim Belushi. A smidge shorter and heavier, but otherwise a doppelgänger. Kevin winked at me and didn't miss a beat in responding, "Of course! Thanks for letting me drop in. I'd be humbled to do a few autographs and pictures for this esteemed crowd."

I felt the weight of his arm around me, ensnaring me in the ensuing chaos before I could escape. With a wicked grin, he pointed at me and said to the woman, "Let me introduce you to Shelley, my press agent. She'll coordinate the details with you."

Oh, hell no. I shot him my best *are you fucking kidding me?* look. Apparently not threatening enough, because he ordered another vodka soda and sauntered off to mingle with the agency crew, leaving me standing with this strange woman to coordinate a very fake autograph session for a very real group of dignitaries. Did I also mention that the press was in the house? I had the choice to tell the truth, and yet, for the sake of my job, I perpetuated the lie. I improvised a corner of the main room into a makeshift autograph table and photo stage for Kevin to work his magic (or his mess.)

Within thirty minutes, a guest at the party, who was a real-life acquaintance of Jim Belushi's, called our bluff, and we were swiftly booted out of the ambassador's residence and blacklisted for life. I was less worried about that than I was about whether we would be on the front page of *Al-Ahram* or *Daily News Egypt* the next morning. Thankfully, we weren't.

My time with the Bribe Tribe and my expulsion from the ambassador's residence were wake-up calls for me. I was putting up with a lot for the sake of advancement, recognition, and acceptance. I might have been a rebel, but I had my limits, and bribery and deceit should have been way past them. They didn't feel like a price I should have to pay for my job. However, I was willing to make sacrifices to stay in Turkey. I wanted to explore more, and mostly, I wanted to be with Candan. Once I knew I could stay for a while, I dove headfirst into our romance. My rebel self loved the idea of an exotic foreign relationship, edgy, against the grain. My soul loved the idea of a mate.

Candan and I became inseparable after that first year. We moved in together. We adventured across Turkey and Europe together. We even worked together until he left the agency for a new job, so our work didn't get in the way of our love. He was the supportive and nurturing half of our partnership. I was the fire and energy. He was the heart. I was the head.

We were from different worlds and different backgrounds. I was so much my driven, executive father and he was so much his huge-hearted, nurturing mother. She was a traditional woman who grew herbs, fruits, and vegetables in an urban garden, cooked every abundant meal from scratch, sewed clothes for the family, and bowed toward Mecca five times a day. She had never traveled outside of Turkey. Her life's work was raising four children, three of whom still lived under her roof and ate meals together most nights of the week. She wanted Candan back home too.

Imagine her reaction when, instead of coming home, he brought an American girlfriend to meet the family. On our way there, Candan warned me that his mom would likely bite me if she liked me. (WTF? There was nothing customary about that—I should've known from the beginning.) Halfway through our first dinner, she clobbered me with a big bear hug and sank her teeth into the meatiest part of my left shoulder. It was an auspicious start to say the least. Candan was a mama's boy, so I believe she initially wanted to love me as much as her son did. But as our relationship became more serious, his mother grew more distant. She struggled to accept that her son had fallen in love with a foreign and nontraditional woman who would potentially take him thousands of miles from home.

And, of course, that's exactly what happened. A couple of years later, her worst nightmare came true when I was recruited to a big strategy job at America Online (AOL) in New York City. It was a no-brainer for me. I was ready to leap into the twenty-first century and the arms of a city in which I had always dreamt of living. I didn't pause to consider settling in Turkey—I was still in hide 'n seek mode. I told Candan I was accepting the job, no matter what. It was his choice whether he wanted to join me or not. Clearly my career was still feeding the rebel. I was following the call, willing to pay almost any price, including my heart.

Soul Search

AUTHENTICITY

1. On a scale from 1 to 10, how authentically are you living your life right now?

> 1 = I've got more masks than a Halloween party.
> 10 = I'm jamming to Lady Gaga's "Born this Way."

> 1   2   3   4   5   6   7   8   9   10

2. What would change if you were being 100 percent true to you right now? List the top three things that immediately spring to mind.

3. If you're being honest, are you chasing your dream or someone else's? Where is that serving you? And what is it costing you? Describe your dream.

4. What's your version of a "Why-dentity"? Where is it coaxing you to play safe and/or fit in?

5. What do you love to do that would reconnect you with your inner rebel? What rules are you dying to break?

6. If you continue to live as you are now for the next three, five, ten, or more years, will you be moving toward who you want to become, or farther away? How does that make you feel? What are you willing to do differently to move in the direction of who you want to become?

S.O.U.L. Process

After spending time reflecting on the questions above, choose one new insight or truth you want to take action on now and follow the S.O.U.L. process below. Use this for as many insights as you want. Lather, rinse, repeat.

S: **Show up.** Commit to having integrity with yourself. Stop hiding and playing safe. State aloud the new truth you want to create in service of your authentic self. (It often starts with "I am_____," "I will_____," or "I can_____.")

O: **Own it.** Repeat the truth again and again until you believe it's possible, and then accept responsibility for making it happen. Evict any competing stories and disempowering language (I can't/I should/I have to) from your mind.

U: **Unleash it.** Put clear intentions into the Universe. Share your truth with those who will support, inspire, and/or mentor you. Take one small step toward what you want to create, and witness the synchronicity that follows. The Universe opens one door at a time.

L: **Live it.** Create boundaries and make conscious choices in service of your new truth. Prioritize it. Get creative. Ditch the excuses. Live the idea of who you want to become, or what you want to create, *before you're ready*.

Section 3:

7.

SHOULD-ING ALL OVER MYSELF

L ife looked shiny on the outside, but over time, it became a real
hot mess on the inside. I sensed the growing void long before
the repetitive nightmare began, but I quashed it valiantly with
work, wine, justifications, more work, more wine, and more justifications. I muscled my way through the resulting illness, divorce,
addiction, and pain. I never slowed down long enough to consider
who or what it was all in service of. Or ask, by the way, *What do I
really want?*

I was shifting from a life of seeking to a life of should-ing. Convincing myself of all the reasons I *should* do things that I wasn't
passionate about. I was doing things that I thought were important
to my family, or society, or even my own nefarious ego. But not to
my soul. I was habitually should-ing all over myself—and paying a
steep price.

It's no coincidence that "should-ing" sounds an awful lot like "shitting" when you say it out loud. They're pretty much the same thing. When we *should* on ourselves we essentially *shit* on ourselves. We undermine our own infinite power and possibility. We gloss over the underlying beliefs and influences driving our actions. We divert precious energy to things (or people) that don't really matter to us.

It's not easy to admit, but I'd been doing this for decades. Glancing in the rearview mirror, there were three big *should*s that nearly destroyed me:

> I *should* get married and have kids.
> I *should* make personal sacrifices for work.
> I *should* stay on the corporate track.

Maybe one of these statements strikes a chord for some of you. Maybe they spark a "holy shit" moment, as your own should-ing comes into focus. Or maybe you won't recognize yourself in those statements, because you're the kind of person who gets her or his "ahas" through stories and experiences. Well, you're in luck, because I've got some stories and some challenges for you.

Should #1: I *Should* Get Married and Have Kids

Because that's what people do, right? Because the Paxton family is as traditional as tartan plaid. They all get married and stay that way "'til death do us part." Because I fell in love with a Turkish guy, and that seemed the easiest way to bring him to the United States to start our new life together. Because family was important to Candan, and he wanted to create our own.

Suffice it to say, I wasn't your typical little girl who dreamt of flowing white gowns and veils and tiered cakes and happily ever

after. (I'm guessing that doesn't surprise you.) Maybe I didn't believe I deserved it. Maybe it was an early statement of my independence. Maybe I was simply too busy architecting fabulous houses and
new worlds with Legos instead of playing with dolls. (When I did
play with Barbies, they were more likely to be getting their hair
chopped off or to be planning a rocking party than chasing Ken
around.) Or maybe, deep down, I was rebelling against the unsettling 1950s-era power dynamic of my parents' relationship. (A rebel
isn't subservient, after all.) Whatever it was, I had never once imagined myself married.

Then it happened, in one transcontinental blur. When the AOL
offer came to me, it was one of the most iconic brands of the digital revolution. I was salivating at the opportunity to be part of the
dot-com boom and get myself a taste of the *Sex and the City* life.
Candan might not have cared about Carrie Bradshaw and her enviable shoe collection, but he shared my passion for adventure, and
had always wanted to live in New York City. So we said yes to AOL,
NYC, and to our next chapter together.

We got engaged in Istanbul a few weeks later, on New Year's
Eve of Y2K. (Yeah, let's bask in the irony of that for a second. I said
yes to "forever" on the eve of the most widely anticipated techno-
logical apocalypse in history. Sounds about right!) Within a month
of our engagement, I was off to start my new job. Candan arrived
a couple of months later. I hadn't really done my homework on the
proper proceedings for a fiancé visa, and, as it turns out, you can't
just import a foreign lover like a Turkish rug. There's a whole bunch
of rigmarole—endless paperwork, background checks, and imposed
wait times. We decided to fast-track to marriage without proper visas.
In true rebel form, we would ask for forgiveness, not for permission.

With my mom's help, we planned a family-only, civil wedding

ceremony. Three months later, Candan and I were married on Dau-fuskie Island, South Carolina. Barefoot on the beach. The ocean as our witness. No pomp and circumstance. No churches or gowns or veils. Only a simple cake (because, my parents) and numerous bot-tles of Raymond Cabernet Sauvignon (because, all of us). You get the picture.

I was wildly in love with Candan in those days, but I also saw engagement and marriage as practical things I *should* do to ease our transition to New York City. Especially with our intensely curi-ous new "friends" at US Immigration and Naturalization Service. Even in 2000, bringing a foreigner from anywhere in the vicinity of the Middle East into the country for more than a quick holiday was a challenge. But nothing compared to post-9/11. Our lives got a whole lot crazier when the World Trade Center, just over two miles from our postage-stamp-sized West Village apartment, was attacked the following year. We were already married, but the naturalization process for anyone from a predominantly Muslim country suddenly became a painfully slow and ever more invasive process. Actually, it felt more like a criminal investigation. Guilt by association, simply because of the preordained religious designation of Muslim stamped on Candan's Turkish birth certificate. He was about as Muslim as I was Catholic, but why the hell should that matter anyway? (I could write a whole book about the US government *should*-ing on inno-cent people, but that's for another time.)

The topic of children, for us, was an even deeper and more complex issue than immigration and naturalization. You see, I'd gotten pregnant about a year after we started dating. (Note to self and readers: Never underestimate the machismo of Turkish sperm. Sorry, Mom.) At the time Candan and I were definitely falling in love with each other, but the future still looked somewhat complicated and uncertain. I was an expat in Istanbul, traveling every week, getting paid to live out my wanderlust fantasies. I loved the excitement of living abroad, but I couldn't yet see myself settling in one place permanently. I was still dreaming of places I hadn't yet visited, like the Far East and South America and the South Pacific. How would a child fit? Could we be a nomadic family? Would I need to stop traveling? Would becoming a mother impact my work and career trajectory? Candan and I mined the depths of these questions, and so many more.

We felt hope and despair and longing and fear. We vacillated from possibility to paralysis on a daily basis. We agonized over the decision for weeks. We believed we weren't ready. We couldn't yet understand that we would never be ready. That's how life works. When the Universe sends you a tidal wave, you learn how to surf. I know that now.

But, in that moment, we didn't pick up our boards. We didn't trust the wave. We chose to duck, hold our breath, and paddle out for the next one. In other words, we terminated the pregnancy. Not a decision either of us took lightly, but one we made with consciousness and intent, and overwhelming sadness. We felt strongly that we had to understand the shape of our own future together before bringing another human into the world. We chose what we believed was best for us in that moment. Regardless of whether I would go back and tell my twenty-eight-year-old self to make that same decision again, I feel grateful that we had a safe and legal choice that so many still don't have twenty-some years later. (Sigh.)

The procedure was performed in a private hospital in Istanbul, ironically called the American Hospital. It was quick and clinical, I think. Anesthesia erased any details of the experience itself from my memory. I only recall feeling gutted, literally and metaphorically, as we stood silently waiting for a taxi to take us home. When the taxi finally arrived, I slipped into the back seat and stared blankly out the window. Candan took charge, giving the driver directions to our apartment in the seaside neighborhood of Bebek. As soon as he said it, we glanced at each other and burst into tears. Bebek. It means "baby" in Turkish. The word alone felt like salt in a fresh and gaping wound.

Once home, we lit candles and created an impromptu memorial service in our garden. We shared an intuition that we had said good-bye to what would have been a little girl. Our little girl. In memoriam we named her Zoe, and asked her spirit to be our guardian angel.

We never told anyone about Zoe. It was one of the many intimate secrets Candan and I would come to share. We firmly believed that it was no one else's business—our lives, our bodies, our choices. But, in the years that followed, Candan voiced regrets. He was longing to be a father in the same way I was longing to see the world. And find myself. And be successful. Spoiler alert: Our hearts were melding, but our deepest desires weren't.

The conversation about kids was sidelined until we moved to Chicago four years later. My career was skyrocketing. Candan's was not. He had been pursuing photography and filmmaking, lifelong passions of his, and was finding it tough to "start over" in his early thirties. He was feeling increasingly rootless and purposeless—and childless—as I was increasingly wed to work. He couldn't imagine living without children, and I was weighing whether I *should* have them simply to make Candan happy.

But work always seemed to get in the way.

Which leads me to Should #2.

Should #2: I *Should* Make Personal Sacrifices for Work

Because I get paid great money. Because I'm lucky to have this job. Because it's what everyone else at the top does. And, because, if I don't go above and beyond, the company may discover that I'm not really that talented or worthy of the role I'm in. Impostor syndrome was raging, my boundaries were crumbling, and my positive role models were few. An insidious combination, for sure. Anyone else know that one?

I'd made innumerable personal sacrifices. So many that the choice to prioritize salary over soul became second nature to me. I wasn't bitter or resentful; my ego was being rewarded with promotions and titles and money. But beneath the surface, my life was running a low-grade fever. My system was compromised, and in constant defense mode. I now understand it as Soul Sickness.

The defining moment for me came in my mid-thirties, when that low-grade fever suddenly became a high-grade, life-threatening illness. I was on the fast track at a well-known global media agency, running the global McDonald's business (yep, ensnared again). One of my clients, George, had been promoted to a senior executive position at McDonald's China in Shanghai. He and I had had a pretty contentious relationship for most of our time working together, but it had recently come to a head. I lost it after yet another insulting exchange with him. I launched a nuclear email late one night after a few cocktails on a business trip in London—to my boss, I thought, but of course it went straight to the client. If memory serves, I might have said something along the lines of, "Jesus Fucking Christ, I'm sick and tired of working with this arrogant douchebag . . ." And that was just the most printable bit. I wasn't proud of the language I used, or that I caved to a knee-jerk reaction instead of waiting until the emotion passed, but I was proud that I had stood in my power. And, crazy enough, it got George's attention. He understood that he had pushed one of his best agency partners to the edge. He not only apologized, he asked my bosses if they would send me to Shanghai to help him turn the business around. Didn't see that coming. It was a lesson in speaking my truth on so many levels (maybe with a little more eloquence next time).

So, naturally, the agency asked me to move to Shanghai for a short stint—and made the offer as generous and irresistible as possible. All expenses paid, additional bonus incentive, take Candan with you, and we'll care for Moka (our little fur baby) while you're gone. Kate, my boss at the time, was a brilliant, get-'er-done senior executive. She could move mountains, and often did. A kindhearted dog lover, Kate was willing to take Moka into her own home, taking all possible excuses off the table before I could even raise them. Except for one she couldn't possibly have known because, despite our friendship outside of the office, I hadn't shared it with anyone. It was too soon, too raw, too scary. Candan and I were trying to get pregnant.

Maybe I was simply trying to make him happy because of the guilt I felt that he had become tethered to the demands of my career. He missed NYC. He missed Istanbul. He'd left film work, his photography business was struggling, and he didn't want to go back to advertising. He lived to take care of Moka and me. He was a nurturer at heart. And he was lonely.

By this time, my biological clock sounded more like the blaring horn of a cruise ship leaving port. Doctors told us pregnancy might be an uphill battle because of my age, my polycystic ovaries, and my weight. I've never been a small woman, but travel and stress and my penchant for eating and drinking all my emotions had really packed on the pounds. I weighed over two hundred pounds. I'd need to get healthy and dial down the stress in my life if I hoped to conceive. A business turnaround situation in Shanghai was not exactly what the doctor ordered.

But I was afraid that I would no longer be seen as valuable within the company if I didn't go. I feared that saying no would somehow jeopardize my future. My ego was on full FOMO freak-out over missing the opportunity to be part of a success story in the fastest growing economy on the planet. At the same time, I worried that Candan might leave me if I didn't slow down and commit to having kids. He never said that explicitly, but it was a powerful story in my head. If he left, who else would be willing to love me? Especially when I was overweight? Was this my last chance at love and happiness and family, even if it scared the shit out of me?

The people-pleaser in me was desperately searching for a win-win, for my company *and* for my husband. We go to China *and* we still try to make a baby. I convinced Candan it was possible. But not once did I reflect on what *I* would choose to do, given my druthers. I knew my decision was out of alignment with my soul, but I was afraid to say no to either of the two loves of my life.

Man, did I pay the price.

A few weeks later, we were characters in the fast-paced action flick that was Shanghai in 2006, two years before the Beijing Olympics, when China would be putting its best public foot forward on the world stage. The speed of development was mind-blowing, almost disturbing. It was like watching time-lapse video, as old alley homes were leveled in a day and new skyscrapers went up in their place within weeks. We watched in fascination and scrambled to soak up the ancient culture—not to mention the twenty-five-cent black-market DVDs—we feared might soon be gone.

I started feeling out of sorts about a month into our stay. Initially we blamed stress. The local business situation was demanding and I was hell-bent on demonstrating quick progress. But as the days passed, I became increasingly more lethargic and nauseous. My stomach was in constant pain. I had a hard time eating anything but bread or rice. Some days I was thankful I didn't have to. (I'm looking at you, chicken feet.)

For a hot second, we thought I might be pregnant. Except that I was losing weight, not gaining weight. I was too stubborn to admit I was really ill or to visit a Chinese doctor. I had a history of gut issues, so I chalked it up to more of the same. I mean, seriously, I was (barely) standing in the birthplace of centuries of Eastern medical wisdom and philosophy, and I refused to surrender. Choosing work over wellness, I pushed through the pain and exhaustion until I fulfilled my obligation to the company many weeks later.

Candan and I had booked ten days of vacation in Southeast Asia as a way to cap off the adventure before heading home. I crawled my way through Cambodia and Thailand. Puked my guts out on the ancient ruins of Angkor Wat. Never left our villa in Phuket. And finally agreed to go to a private hospital in Bangkok. The doctors couldn't immediately diagnose what was wrong, but they were concerned by my blood work. They wanted to admit me for extensive testing. But if I was going to be in the hospital, I wanted to be near my family, not in Thailand.

Against medical advice, and with two hospital-prescribed tranquilizers in hand, we made the most arduous thirty-six-hour journey of our lives, from Bangkok to Shanghai to Tokyo and, finally, to sweet home Chicago. I don't remember a single minute of it. Only that we got off the last flight and went straight to the emergency room at Northwestern Memorial Hospital in downtown Chicago.

The next two months were a whirlwind of tests. I had become one of those medical mysteries that you read about. A patient who is clearly ill—I was in constant pain, unable to eat more than plain Greek yogurt, and losing weight rapidly—and yet with no clear medical reason why. I was passed from infectious diseases to gastroenterology to neurology, until the doctors at Northwestern finally gave up and sent me up to the famed Mayo Clinic in Rochester, Minnesota, which lived up to its stellar reputation.

Their integrated team of doctors diagnosed me with a bacterial infection that had slowly taken over my entire digestive system. They suspected I might have eaten tainted shrimp from the South China Sea. (So gross, right? It ruined shrimp for me for years.) But, the truth is, we'll never know what caused it. Only that it had gone on for so long that my gallbladder, stomach, and intestines needed a full reboot. The reboot treatment was like a gastrointestinal chemo, a toxic cocktail of drugs whose job it was to attack and eliminate the nasty bacteria in my gut. Of course, in doing so, it also wiped out much of the good gut flora, critical for healthy digestion. So, in between rounds of toxic teardown, I would take prebiotics, probiotics, and other good guys to reestablish a healthy ecosystem of microorganisms. Several grueling rounds later, my system achieved some semblance of normalcy. It took nearly ten months for me to be able to eat and drink all the things I loved again. I'd surgically sacrificed my gallbladder, and was shocked when I figured out I'd lost eighty pounds from start to finish. For the record, it wasn't like those extreme weight loss reality shows where the winners lose ridiculous amounts of weight and their skin shrinks right back into place like the perfect pair of leggings. I didn't emerge looking like a model on the cover of *Shape* magazine. Instead I had loose skin hanging off my frame, like a body pillow with the stuffing pulled out. A perfectly imperfect new form of me. It's not a diet plan I would recommend to anyone, but clearly the Universe put me on it for a reason. Because I wasn't paying attention. And I certainly wasn't prioritizing what really mattered. (Hello, health.)

Coming out the other side, I felt like I had a new lease on life. It's funny, I didn't technically have what you would call a near-death experience, but I know for sure I had what I would call a lack-of-life experience. Scary in its own right. So many of the things I cherished—my energy, vitality, appetite, and freedom—were decimated. I never wanted to feel that way again. I wouldn't let it happen. I was determined to change my life.

I was willing to question everything—marriage, children, lifestyle, and work. I immediately started taking better care of myself—eating healthier, drinking less, and becoming obsessed with kickboxing and boot camp workouts. I put the kibosh on having children, reasoning that a pregnancy might put my just-barely-recovered body through hell. I wasn't willing to go there. I wanted to be strong and healthy, not sick and fat again. (My ego made this a very clear and nonnegotiable distinction. Not sure my soul was invited to the conversation.)

Perhaps more significant, I couldn't imagine shouldering all the responsibility for our livelihood, from mothering to moneymaking, myself. I was already growing resentful. I wanted a partnership where we were both contributing, both living our best lives and inspiring each other to grow in abundance as individuals and as a couple. Perhaps selfishly, I wanted some wiggle room to play, pursue my passions, and maybe even discover my purpose along the way.

We were at an impasse. Candan was living in the past, anchored to what could have been, pining for biological children, abandoning hope for his business, and rapidly losing faith in the American promise of life, liberty, and freedom for all. I was fast-forwarding to the future, trying to catch the winds of what could be, and fantasizing about a passionate relationship with a confident and successful man. That fantasy almost became an affair, with someone I still adore to this day. But, if our relationship was going to end, I wanted it to be clean.

As a last resort, we agreed to marriage counseling. On our third session, the therapist asked us point-blank if we were interested in investing in the relationship. She concluded, "You haven't given me any reasons to believe that you are willing to make this work. There's not an ounce of warmth between you."

You could hear the sound of our hearts breaking in the silence that followed. We had defied the odds for more than ten years. Our love might have been rare and unexpected, but, in the end, it was just as fragile as everyone else's. We had grown apart, not together. The devastating reality settled in like a fog. It was the beginning of the end.

I wish I could tell you that we took the high road. That we were early pioneers of the "conscious uncoupling" movement. Or at least that we're still friends today. Instead, our divorce was a batten-down-the-hatches, hurricane-grade shit storm.

I'll spare you the details, because this is only a single mile marker on a long journey. And you're only hearing my side of a complicated and emotional story. Suffice it to say that mediation, and the desire for an amicable settlement, was abandoned after we couldn't agree on terms. Divorce papers were served, expensive lawyers engaged. Civility was thrown out like the baby with the bathwater. Accusations were launched, mail was stopped, credit cards went unpaid, phones were broken into, and judges became referees. And this storm raged for over a year, in which I helplessly watched its fury batter my hard-earned retirement and investment accounts.

Work was a safe haven. So I put in long hours and traveled as often as possible to escape the lethal flying debris of my newly splin-tered life. To be honest, I hated coming home. Lines of battle had been drawn in our loft—his side and my side—because a fight for ownership kept us squatting in the same home. Shared spaces were awkward and uncomfortable. So I withdrew to my bedroom, and the inside of my head. I wanted to stay strong, but I was losing hope that there would be anything left when the storm was over. So much of our money was going toward legal fees, and an allowance for Can-dan to maintain his "quality of life." I was terrified that everything for which I had sacrificed my life and health for nearly twenty years would be leveled in the storm.

I quickly spiraled into depression. But I didn't tell anyone. Or ask for help of any kind. Sadly, there I was, a well-educated, thirty-eight-year-old senior executive, unable to step into the vulnerability required to ask for help. I didn't know how to go there. I didn't have any training or role models. I kept my feelings down and my guard up, telling everyone the situation was tough, but I was "hanging in there." Those words alone were a cry for help. But no one heard it, because my armor was spit-polished to a deceptive shine.

Until one Saturday morning, halfway through my favorite boot camp class at the local gym, I walked out. I had forced myself to go in hopes that exercise would get me out of my head, but the dark tape kept playing, *Why are you even bothering? This isn't going to make the pain go away.* I believed there was only one thing that would.

Candan was gone when I got home. He had said something about being away for most of the day. In his absence, the loft was unusually still, almost peaceful. I was craving peace from the depths of my soul. I wanted so desperately to be done with the vitriol, the hatred, the games, the lawyers, and the masking tape line down the middle of my life. I wanted to be done.

In a zombie-like state of surrender, I walked into my bedroom and locked the door behind me. I gathered all the prescription medication in my bathroom. There was still a lot of potent stuff from the days of the Mayo Clinic. This was my plan B. I didn't write a note. I didn't even change out of my gym clothes. I determinedly swallowed pill after pill after pill. Believing, hoping, praying that the combination would be lethal enough to usher me into peace. Forever.

Then I tucked myself back into bed and whispered into the Universe, "Goodbye. I love you, Mom, Dad, and Christy. Please forgive me."

Clearly that didn't go as planned. Candan foiled my plans (again). I hated him for it at the time, but am now eternally grateful for the series of events that led him to come home early, try to get my attention, and finally follow his intuition to break into the bedroom when I was unresponsive for an hour. He got me to the hospital just in time to save my life.

I woke up the next day to my mom sitting bedside, tenderly stroking my hair and kissing my face. Telling me over and over again how much she loved me. My sister was there, too. Stewing in sadness and anger, mad as hell that I tried to leave this planet without first calling my family or a friend or even a suicide prevention hotline. And she was right (for once).

I paid my penance over the next couple of weeks: twenty-four-seven suicide watch in the hospital, a guard shadowing me to protect me from myself, and a one-week mental health assessment in the psych ward. The whole experience was frustrating and claustrophobic, but hugely enlightening. I realized I already had access to the freedom I was seeking. In life, not in death.

The point of my sharing this story isn't to drag you through the gory details or the living hell that is a psychiatric ward when you're not really crazy. The purpose is for me to finally say out loud to the world, "I tried to kill myself, and I'm so happy I survived." I got a second chance, just like my dad. There *is* hope, and there *are* options. Until this book, I've only ever shared what I did with ten or so people, including my family. I never even told work what really happened. Kate and the crew at the agency believed that I had a serious relapse from the bacterial infection. Because that's what I wanted them to believe. They had been so incredibly supportive through the illness and the divorce; I didn't want them to know how weak I'd really become.

I've carried around so much shame related to trying to take my own life. Shame for believing that I had to end it all to find peace. Shame for not seeking support. Massive shame for not talking about it publicly and bringing hope to others.

As of now, I'm releasing that shame by naming it and shining a white-hot spotlight on it. (Thank you, Brené.) I am stepping out to own it so that my story may help to liberate even one soul from the depths of despair. I'm committed to increasing my contribution to the work of mental health and suicide prevention. Several years after my own attempt, I lost a dear friend to suicide, David Price. We shared a birthday and a soul. And then, at thirty-one years young, he was gone. I experienced what it feels like on the other side of this kind of senseless loss.

I turned forty in the best health and shape of my life, save for a few hearty battle scars. I'd survived the divorce but, sadly, lost Moka in the cross fire as well. I had always believed he was the guardian angel of our relationship. He nuzzled his way into our lives a week before the wedding and, staying painfully true to script, started to check out as tensions escalated and Candan returned to Turkey. He was already blind and struggling with a few substantial health issues when Candan left, but three weeks prior to the final court date, the vet called me at work to say, "Moka won't be coming home. His organs are failing. It's time to let him go." I raced to the clinic to kiss his wrinkly little manatee face one last time.

Sitting on the floor of the examination room, in a pool of my own mascara-stained tears and snot, I felt so alone. Everything was coming to an end at once. It was too much. I watched helplessly as they swaddled my baby in blankets and prepared him to be euthanized in my arms. In that moment, I thought of Candan and his devotion to Moka. He loved him so dearly, and would want the chance to say goodbye. It was time to take the high road. I rang his mobile phone.

It was the middle of the night in Istanbul, but Candan picked up. My words were barely intelligible, desperate wails that shook the line. There was silence on the other end. Then sobbing. He understood. We cried together. For a moment, I thought the devastating intimacy of the experience would bring some level of closure between us. Finally, some peace.

And then I heard the voice of a man I once loved spit out like venom: "You killed our dog like you killed our marriage."

Click.

I'm a pretty smart girl, but the Universe gave me a serious smackdown, and it seems I only got part of the lesson. Other people get sick, almost die, and make significant life changes. I changed many things, but not my work. I considered it an acceptable (even necessary) price to pay, especially after the financial devastation of the divorce. I knew I was sitting on a rusty nail but, as the old adage goes, it just didn't hurt badly enough yet to get off it.

Which leads me to Should #3.

Should #3: I *Should* Stay on the Corporate Track

Because, my dad. Because I've sunk in so much time and energy. Because, a very comfortable lifestyle. Because it's too late/I'm too old to pivot to something new and succeed. Even as I write these words, I'm embarrassed by how privileged they sound. I'm humbly aware of how much good fortune has come my way in this lifetime, and I'm also aware of how hard I've worked for the chance to enjoy and grow it. Every experience I've had has led to where I'm standing today, shouting from this gorgeous mountaintop.

But that's not really the point. The point is that I had been questioning my purpose and path from the ripe young age of twenty-six (remember my first Soulbbatical?), and I didn't do anything about it until the just-shy-of-mid-life-crisis-awakening age of forty-six. Twenty freaking years later. For all those years I was telling myself, "I *should* make it work. This is what I'm good at, even if it doesn't make me happy." I got trapped in the vicious self-imprisonment cycles of "I'll be happy when . . ." and "Things will get better if . . ." chasing money, titles, passport stamps, and material things that I didn't want nearly as much as I wanted to believe they would somehow make me feel whole, more alive inside, like all the sacrifice had somehow been worth it. Of course, we can never get enough of what we don't really need, right?

It turns out I was living my dad's dream. Sprinting up the corporate ladder. Earning my first VP title by the age of thirty-two. Getting hooked on the adrenaline and adventure and opportunity. Always looking upward, rarely inward. Forsaking self-worth for net worth.

When I was young, I thought I would be an architect or a designer. I loved to create things from my imagination, and invent stories to give them context. I constructed miniature-scale eccentric modern houses, avant-garde furniture, and colorful new worlds from Lego and balsa wood, wildly different from the cookie-cutter subdivisions in which I was being raised. It's so clear to me now that I was creating the world I wanted to live in. It seems I was a Rebel Soul Architect from a young age. Forty-odd years later, I'm fully living that dream in a vibrant city, designed by some of the world's most famous architects. My home and headquarters is a historic urban loft converted from an old garment factory, with massive nine-pane windows, timber ceilings, brick walls, sporting the original steel doors. And lots of mid-century modern décor. It's my happy place. The place from which I live my best life—and help my clients do the same.

But, that's jumping way ahead in the story. We're now post-divorce, and I still haven't woken up to what my soul and the Universe have been conspiring to help me understand. My mom tells me that as a kid I would have to hit my head against a wall at least three times until I would get (or accept) any lesson. Some things never change. I could be a stubborn mo-fo, for sure. Especially when my ego was being wooed.

I was settling into the rhythm of my new life after a promotion, and leading a new global digital strategy group. I liked the work, and it gave me time to focus on my health. I even began wading into the dating pool after a self-imposed, nine-month "get your shit together" man ban. (Side note: This girl hadn't been on a first date since 1997, the dawn of the Internet, so a few things had changed. Wading might have looked a bit more like flailing, in my case.) I met a solid guy through mutual friends in the real world and we were about four months into our relationship when, on a business trip to New York City, I got a text from Mark-Hans saying he needed to see me when he was in Chicago later that week. He seemed insistent, and since it had been a while since we'd seen each other, my brain bypassed reason and leapt straight to catastrophe: *Holy shit, he's getting divorced, too! Or he's dying!* I knew he had gone to Harley-Davidson a couple of years prior to become their first chief marketing officer, but it didn't even occur to me that he might try to recruit me. Hell, I wasn't even a rider.

A few days later, I landed at O'Hare airport and went straight to the downtown bar to meet Mark-Hans. I found him in the back, drinking beer and laughing with a couple of his old buddies. He looked well and happy. But, then he excused his friends abruptly so we could have a private conversation, and paranoia tackled me again. Before he could finish his first sentence, I grabbed him and blurted out, "Please, please tell me you're okay!" He quickly put two and two together and burst out laughing, nearly falling off the barstool. "I'm more than okay, Shel. I have a gorgeous wife, two beautiful daughters, and I run marketing for Harley-fucking-Davidson. I have the best job on the planet."

Pause.

"And I want you to join me."

"Whaaaaaaaaaaaat?" My insides kicked into a spin cycle of elation, gratitude, surprise, terror, confusion, and amazement. I couldn't find words to articulate everything I was feeling, so my mouth landed on an ineloquent version of the truth, "Really? Me? Why?" *Awesome sales pitch, Shelley.*

But he already knew the answer. He had written the job spec himself. He knew exactly who and what he needed to build a world-class marketing organization. Someone with significant global experience and a fresh perspective on the industry. He needed a strong leader who would stand up to the prevailing culture and agitate for change. He needed someone who could authentically represent the brand and earn the respect of customers, dealers, and teams around the world.

He needed me.

I was wildly flattered, and deeply conflicted. I was finally getting my life back on the rails. I loved Chicago. I was having fun dating the new guy. We were spending a lot of time together—so much so that I ditched my perennial "It's Complicated" Facebook status. Things felt in flow for the first time in years. But I couldn't resist the allure of a rebel brand, even if it meant disrupting my own stability and a promising relationship. When would I ever get this chance again?

I could already hear my dad's voice in my head: "You'd be nuts to pass it up. It's a chance to become senior management at a Fortune 500 company. Of course, you *should* do it!"

I didn't know anyone in Milwaukee. I had never even been there before my first visit to Harley. And my boyfriend couldn't move to Milwaukee because he had two young daughters from a previous marriage living in the Chicago suburbs. But I jumped into the interview process anyway, and found myself accepting a job as VP, Integrated Marketing + Planning a couple of months later.

I had created the perfect system for sabotaging my own peace and happiness. There I was again, pulling the pin and launching the grenade. But I couldn't see that at the time. I reasoned that I could make a long-ish distance relationship work since Milwaukee and Chicago were only ninety miles apart. And I'd lived all over the world, so why not take a chance on Milwaukee? More than anything, I wanted to prove to the world and myself that, after being rocked by illness and divorce, I was more badass than ever; that my next chapter would be epic. The world would know that Shelley

Paxton was back in her rebel prime. I straddled the iron horse, got my license, and rolled on the throttle.

It was the ride of a lifetime in many respects. Within four weeks of joining the company I was on a plane to European Bike Week in Faak am See, Austria. Riding with colleagues and customers across the Alps into Italy and Slovenia. Experiencing the most powerful and loyal community of humans and riders in the world. Bonding in a way that transcended languages and borders. Living the essence of a brand customers loved so deeply they tattooed it on their bodies. Harley-Davidson was an international icon of freedom and rebellion and individuality. These were my people.

I experienced this again and again in Brazil, Mexico, South Africa, Spain, Italy, France, India, Japan, Canada, England, Australia, the US, and so many other countries. Harley events in the mountains, by the sea, on the plains, and smack-dab in the middle of some of the world's most beautiful cities. (And so we meet again, Barcelona.)

One of the most memorable experiences was our 110th anniversary event in Rome. The Vatican agreed to a first-ever Papal Bike Blessing in Saint Peter's Square. Bike Blessings are a tradition in motorcycling, usually held in early summer, with the intention of bringing safety and good fortune for the riding season. They're typically done at places of worship in local communities, not in Rome with the freaking pope. On that Sunday morning in June, thousands of bikes and riders lined the road leading up to Saint Peter's Square. The anticipation of the crowd was like the buzz of a million bees. Press was everywhere capturing the historic moment. And when Pope Francis came out to bless the bikes, the thunderous roar of thousands of V-twin engines being revved in unison shook the walls of the ancient city.

Well, that's how it felt anyway. From afar. Because, after a year of planning, months of excruciating negotiations with the Vatican, and hours of parking bikes in the scorching Roman sun, Mark-Hans and I missed the actual blessing. And it was my fault. I had asked him to join me for a quick coffee and breakfast away from the square. We had no idea when the pope would do the actual blessing—we only knew it would be sometime before or after his ritual public mass. I made sure to have a walkie-talkie with me at breakfast so the team could radio at any sighting of the pope. But I forgot to turn the volume on. For real.

I considered it a week of miracles: I didn't get fired from Harley-Davidson after causing my boss to miss a once-in-a-lifetime event. And, the day before, in a private meeting with Pope Francis, I shook his hand without lightning striking. It was almost enough to make this recovering Catholic into a believer.

Harley-Davidson was in growth mode for many of my years there, focused on aggressive international expansion and bringing innovative new products to market in order to attract new riders and new customer segments. My team was leading the global launch of Street, H-D's first smaller bikes for newer and more price sensitive riders, and the initial introduction of LiveWire, H-D's first electric motorcycle. The latter was so noteworthy it was written up in a spread in *Time* magazine. We were on a roll.

But, that was the filtered Instagram version of my life. Reality was somewhat darker and less enviable. Behind the epic events and product launches and global travel lay an increasingly unhealthy relationship with work. My boundaries had collapsed again. I was working long hours and weekends, and traveling for significant periods of time. I was drained by a culture where multiday meetings were the norm and leaders bragged about not taking vacation. We worked on factory hours, and across every time zone, so nearly every day started at 6:30 or 7:00 A.M. and ended around 9:00 or 10:00 P.M. And, as sales slowed around 2014, we got thrown into a vicious cycle of annual reorganizations. It was a nauseating merry-go-round of shifting priorities, restructuring, letting people go, implementing new plans and then restructuring again before progress could take hold. Along the way, I took on responsibility for the entire marketing organization, and watched Mark-Hans and several other senior leaders who were fighting the good fight get shown the door. It felt to me like we had lost touch with what made Harley-Davidson so great in the first place—authenticity, community, and rebellion.

I know a lot of this isn't unique to Harley. And that's the point. We put up with cultures that are soul-sucking instead of demanding cultures that are soul-filling. As you know, I'm passionate about liberating the soul of business as well. Read to the end, and let's figure out how to remedy this together.

Unfortunately, my personal life was also in the shitter. The Chicago romance imploded after about eighteen months. Distance wasn't necessarily the culprit, but it did expose the cracks in our foundation. We didn't share the same values or vision for the future. But, I had fallen hard for his daughters. I didn't want to leave them. I wasn't their mom, but I got a taste for what it feels like to make a real impact in a child's life. And I loved it. It surfaced a deep maternal instinct and longing I had never known. At the just-beyond-ripe age of forty-two.

Then, as if on cue, I met a man who rocked my world and almost became father to my child. He was many years my junior and yet the oldest soul with whom I'd ever connected. We spoke about Rumi and Hafiz and the Stoic philosophers. We dreamt about traveling the world together, creating a contrarian life. Our love was sacred and passionate and otherworldly. It was also an impossible fantasy. We used to jokingly end our conversations with the words "for now" as if we knew it couldn't last. He lived in another country. He wanted marriage and kids. We got to see each other only four times a year, when work or a romantic rendezvous would bring us together. Taking a chance on our love felt too risky for both of us. It meant weighty career decisions, moving our lives, and, for him, taking a gamble on a relationship that might never bear children. We decided to end the affair. It was devastating, but it was our choice. Almost immediately, he became engaged to marry a much younger woman. At the same time, I discovered that I had been pregnant with, and miscarried, his child.

From that point on I associated love with loss. It was all I'd known. I believed that I was unlovable or, at the very least, incapable of creating a healthy relationship. I had no idea who or what I really wanted. I was simply lonely and attempting to fill a void. So I tried online dating (again) and even matchmaking services. I dated older guys and way-too-young-for-me guys. I dated brown guys and white guys, American guys and foreign guys, business guys and creative guys, faithful guys and unfaithful guys. I was sometimes the main course, and often the side dish. I was called a "force of nature" and "fascinating" and "fun" and "witty and brilliant" and even "sexy." One asshole called me "thick" (as in heavy, not stupid). Ouch. But nothing ever lasted long enough to be called "partner." I was intimidating and unavailable—always looking for the exit. My heart was shielded by the same armor I carried to work every day.

And I was attracting that same energy into my life.

It's true what they say in business—that it's lonely at the top. Even lonelier when you don't have a partner at home with whom to share your wins and losses and dreams and fears and dirty little secrets. My partner was my work, and that felt painfully lopsided. I started to wonder if being a strong, independent, and successful woman necessarily meant being alone for the rest of my life.

I continued to believe I should make the choice to stay on the corporate track. That I should push through the pain instead of trying to understand it. And that led to a(nother) cycle of weight gain and numbing. When I wrote about the Moka nightmare in the opening chapter, I mentioned I was sucking down bottles of wine like they were water, at least a bottle a night. I always said I loved wine, but I don't think I could even taste it anymore. I only wanted the feeling of less pain. I was over-drinking to feel numb. I was overeating to fill a void. And I was over-exercising to counter the first two, as well as maintain a shred of sanity. Everything in my world was becoming extreme.

I was paying the price for being so far out of alignment with myself. This is when the nightmare started, and the awakening began.

8.

LIBERATING FROM THE SHACKLES OF SHOULD

Even the coolest job can burn you out. I am living proof. It would be easy to blame Harley-Davidson and its propagation of armored leadership (as Brené would call it), but my choices were my choices. I chose to stay and play the way I did for six and a half years. I believed I could make a difference—and I did.

But there was a dark side as well.

I was one of only six women in the executive ranks of a Fortune 500 company, in a very male-dominated industry. I wanted to prove what a badass I was, so I consciously made immense sacrifices for the sake of salary. I was aware that the unspoken expectations included long hours, endless meetings, weekend travel, and nearly twenty-four-seven availability. The bigger the paycheck, the more substantial the sacrifices. I was firmly in the grip of the golden handcuffs—or, as I called them, the "Shackles of Should."

So you know what I did to justify it all and make myself feel (er, look) better? I glammed up the armor: Jimmy Choo handbags, Christian Louboutin shoes, Alexis Bittar jewelry, and even an insanely expensive Azzedine Alaïa dress from Barneys that made me feel like the queen I longed to be.

Warning: Objects in the rearview mirror may appear shinier than they actually are.

Inside I wrestled with feelings of loneliness and disappointment, secretly wondering if this was all there was at the top of the corporate ladder—life-threatening stress, precious little oxygen, and fulfillment as fleeting as good weather at the summit of Everest. Had I missed the point? Was the climb about the badge and the status more than the experience itself? Was the goal to simply survive in order to prove to ourselves (and possibly others) that we could do it? That didn't feel soul-filling to me at all.

It hadn't yet struck me that I might be climbing the wrong mountain.

In my heart, I believed I could make the company a better place for my team. I wanted to pioneer the example for what wholehearted leadership and culture could look like. So I did what I always did. I pushed through, forged ahead, and fought like hell. That was exactly the kind of language I used too. I read it now and hear how aggression, masculinity, and struggle pervaded every part of my life. I was a Warrior. Not until I came into alignment with my soul would I have access to my true leadership powers: vulnerability, femininity, and raw courage.

So if you're getting a little niggling feeling in your gut, promise me you'll give it some attention. Explore it. Listen to it before the Universe intervenes with illness, loss, or other trauma. Before you regret not doing that difficult thing because it felt too scary or made you feel too vulnerable. I'm sharing my story because every step of my beautiful career led me to this place; to be your soul guide on a journey that took me so long to understand on my own. This is your chance to catch yourself and pivot. Make the changes you want before the foundation crumbles and you're forced to make changes anyway.

Okay, let's take our soul pact to a whole new level with some white-hot truth. How many of you have ever found yourself hoping (or praying) that something will happen that'll make your decision easier? Like silently pleading with the Universe that maybe you'll get cut in the next round of layoffs or you'll be passed over for the next promotion or your partner will tell you to just "go for it"? I'm raising my hand on that one too. There were definitely times that I prayed that someone else would make the decision for me, instead of my having to step up and be true to myself. We do this because we're wired to avoid the hard things—until we're not. Until living our lives in such misalignment finally becomes unsustainable.

So, listen up: Stop pretending your dreams are a "maybe" or a "one-day" or, even worse, a nonstarter. Be honest and bold. Be the person who takes the path less traveled, and defiantly put your soul goals ahead of all else, perhaps for the first time ever. Do now what I was afraid to do for years.

The vicious cycle continued throughout my Harley years—weight gain (again), addiction to numbing with food and booze (again), and stomach issues (again). Chronic coughing and bronchitis were thrown into the mix like an unexpected left jab from the Universe. I've always known that I have strong gut instincts when it comes to business and yet, ironically, I ignored my own gut on a personal level constantly. I lived on wine, antibiotics, Imodium and Pepto-Bismol. Not exactly the breakfast (or lunch or dinner) of champions.

I convinced myself that short-term fixes would help. Twice a year, I embarked on a monthlong detox to reset my system. I'd commit short-term to some version of a clean diet that would eliminate all my addictions for those thirty days: no caffeine, no sugar, no alcohol, no gluten, and no dairy. After a few days of withdrawal, I would inevitably feel like the best version of myself thanks to deep restful sleep, phenomenal energy, and blissful clearheadedness. Oh, and weight loss, of course. During these times, I also noticed that I would defend my boundaries and personal priorities like a Viking. It's amazing how you begin to respect yourself again when self-care makes it to the top of the to-do list.

But, like clockwork, on day thirty-one, I would unwittingly slip back into the comforting arms of my toxic loves. I would laughingly say to friends and colleagues, "I detox so I can retox." It was such a running joke at Harley that I almost had T-shirts made to commemorate the phrase. We laughed because we knew the truth: retoxing not only had to do with what we were consuming but also the environment that was consuming us. We were choosing to poison ourselves from the inside out and the outside in. It was challenging to correct one without the other. I didn't fully understand that to make lasting change—a true soul detox—I had to be willing to upgrade my mind-set, behaviors, *and* environment. Not easy but life changing, as I came to find out.

When it comes to how we live, there's a lot of conversation around the notion of balance. The phrase "work-life balance" is bandied about like a magical elixir that will cure the seemingly conflicting priorities that plague us. To be honest, this idea of having two opposing lives that require precarious balance has always felt to me like a strange juxtaposition, a setup for failure. Most of us, after all, have one holistic "life," with multiple dimensions: family, work, spiritual, social, fitness, etc. So, what if we thought about our lives in terms of alignment versus balance? What if we made decisions based on what aligns with our most important (soul) priorities instead of pushing those to the bottom of the list so often? Even more radical, what if we thought about our days in terms of energy management instead of time management?

These decisions will also inspire boundaries to protect and celebrate family time, soul time, sleep time, playtime, and healthy routines. And to minimize the energy-sucking encroachment of email, meetings, constant accessibility, and over-yessing to things we feel a sense of guilt or obligation to do (more on that to come).

Alignment comes from being true to who you are and what you want. From getting clear on your values. From choosing to do the things, and be with the people, that create real joy and fulfillment in all aspects of your life. From releasing the "shoulds" and "have tos" in favor of the "want tos" and "get tos." Language and intention matter.

Our one precious life can be aligned to Soul Fuels or Soul Sucks, or some combination of the two. If you've never thought about it in these terms, it's profoundly revealing. Imagine this: A blank sheet of paper with the title My Life at the top. The rest of the page is divided into two columns—Soul Fuels on the left and Soul Sucks on the right. Think of Soul Fuels as the people, places, and activities that set your soul on fire. Those things that make your soul feel like a water balloon on the slippery verge of bursting with joy. Soul Sucks are the exact opposite. They're the heavy wet blankets of self-doubt, perceived obligation, toxic relationships, and, of course, the litany of shoulds. Those things that suck the oxygen out of your fire and are guaranteed to burst your balloon.

Now take that piece of paper and spend fifteen minutes in stream-of-consciousness flow, writing everything you can think of in each column. No judgment, no editing, no stopping. When the time is up, pull back slowly and experience both lists. Which one is longer? What surprises you? What alarms you? What emotions do the lists bring up for you?

If the Soul Sucks column is substantially longer than the Soul Fuels one (and for many of us, it is), it's no wonder you're cranky, exhausted, unfulfilled, and burnt out. Then the big questions become unavoidable: What are you willing to do to shift the balance? How will you eliminate the major Soul Sucks in favor of inviting more Soul Fuels into your life? How courageous will you be in choosing the things that truly set your soul on fire and prioritize alignment in your life?

Acting on these choices is challenging. It takes focus and commitment and conviction to stay the course. You know what they say—the right thing is rarely the easy thing.

It certainly wasn't for me. Not one bit of leaving a twenty-six-year career at the peak of my game was easy. It required a formal resignation from all I believed I was—my paycheck, title, and certified badass status—in service of who I would become.

While I knew it was the absolute right decision for me, I wanted to make sure it was a win for Harley-Davidson as well. Not only because I thought it was the right thing to do but because I sincerely loved the brand and the hundreds of marketing people around the world behind it. They were, and still are, the most passionate collection of humans I know. I wanted to leave them in good hands, with as bright a future as I could help architect. The timing of my departure became critical when we embarked on yet another significant reorganization (it's an annual holiday event, as anyone at the company will joke). I understood my choice in that moment: lead through the re-org and beyond *or* design the most optimal organization and leave it in the best shape possible with a powerful successor. I chose the latter. And it happened quickly.

I vividly remember the Friday morning I walked into my boss's office and turned a re-org update into an emotional resignation. I had been planning the moment for two weeks, getting pep talks from my financial advisor and executive coach so I wouldn't lose my nerve. I'd been warning my family that this was going to happen, with or without their support. Like many people, my parents thought I was crazy. They're from the baby boomer generation, which largely operates out of scarcity. They were taught never to leave one job without having another lined up. Even worse, they couldn't imagine walking away from traditional success for something as vague as the liberation of one's soul. The chorus of "You're doing *what*?" and "Are you *sure*?" and "You could totally get another *job*" was deafening. I was grasping for earplugs. But I wasn't deterred.

The tears rolled from the second I sat down at the table in my boss's office, and he instinctively knew to simply listen and hold space for me. It felt so raw. I was scared shitless. My soul had my ego in a choke hold. She was in charge of this one, and didn't care about letting the masks fall. The words were going to come out however they were meant to come out. And so they did, in a way I could never have rehearsed. Not unlike twenty years earlier when I was requesting my first Soulbbatical.

"Paul, I love Harley. You know how much I love Harley. And I know how much Harley loves me. But we aren't growing together. We aren't as happy together anymore. My soul feels like it's dying, which seems crazy to say while working for one of the most soulful brands in the world. But, it's how I feel. I just don't see a future to-gether. It's time for me to go be Shelley Paxton in the world. What-ever that looks like and however scary it may be."

Long pause. Deep breath.

"Please don't make a counteroffer—my decision is final."

In the delirious outpouring of my desires, I also said I was going to write a book. Little did I know it would be the story of this mo-mentous decision and the transformational journey that followed.

At the time it felt like a second divorce—painful, emotional, and liberating as fuck. I'm pretty sure I heard the distinct metallic sound of the Shackles of Should hitting the floor as I walked out the door.

The phrase "get out of your comfort zone" has become a cliché, but there's a reason it's so powerful. When we choose courage over comfort, we choose growth and authenticity. As author John C. Maxwell says, "Change is inevitable. Growth is optional." Letting go of what's no longer serving us, from toxic relationships to self-doubt to fear, is the foundation to living your best life. You will never have all the an-swers or all the confidence (believe me, I still don't!). But letting go anyway, and trusting the Universe, creates space for what's to come and what's meant to be. One of my personal mantras is "Letting go is letting grow." Feel free to steal it if it works for you.

Following your soul is also about asking for what you want. That idea may feel impossible at times, but don't let the resistance stop you. And don't ask for permission, pretty please. You are the Chief Soul Officer of your own life. You have a lifetime supply of pink permission slips (remember those from grade school?) for whatever your soul desires. Use them liberally to pursue whatever joy and fulfillment you want to achieve.

In my case, I didn't ask to negotiate with Harley-Davidson. I finally came to terms with the fact that Harley couldn't give me what I most wanted: freedom to be me. So I asked the Universe for support and guidance.

Maya Angelou once wrote, "Life is not measured by the number of breaths we take, but by the moments that take our breath away." Amen. That describes the moment I walked out of Harley-Davidson headquarters in Milwaukee in September 2016. Despite two weighty boxes of motorcycle memories in my arms, I floated to my car. It was a gorgeous summer day and I was heading to meet a dear friend (and now, former colleague) for an alfresco lunch at a favorite café in the Third Ward. We spent the next hour celebrating, laughing hysterically at the crazy times we'd endured together. I remember Chris asking with envy, "So, you're free. What are you going to do now?"

"I have no fucking idea," I responded as I raised my glass of sauvignon blanc to his Belgian pilsner.

And then it was over.

He rushed back to his next marathon meeting.

I was alone at 1:00 P.M. on a Friday, with nowhere else to go. So, I ordered another glass of wine and people-watched, with the curiosity of a social anthropologist.

What do free people do on a weekday afternoon?

How do free animals live?

How domesticated have I actually become?

I took notes on my brethren in the wild, wondering how I could build up my powerful huntress muscles again.

Day one of my new life was actually day four. I had walked out of Harley the Friday before Labor Day weekend, so the first three days felt, well, like any long holiday weekend: fabulously fun and full of cocktails. Monday night I became aware of a new sensation, an un-expected levity. I wasn't dreading the next morning. My stomach wasn't cramping. I wasn't drunk.

Then Tuesday morning hit. Everyone else went back to work, except me. I didn't know what to do with myself, or what to call myself. I had a Soul Contract in hand with no instructions. Not even the impossible-to-interpret IKEA kind. And this was going to re-quire more than an Allen wrench to get the job done.

That first I-don't-have-a-job-anymore morning was a delirious combination of "Why doesn't everyone do this?" and "What the fuck have I done?" I remember sitting on my balcony, staring out at the Milwaukee River, coffee in hand, feeling almost paralyzed by the lack of structure. I was so used to the incessant busy-ness of meet-ings from 7:00 A.M. to 10:00 P.M. Stillness made me anxious.

Halfway through a pot of coffee, I fired up my laptop and logged into LinkedIn, the arbiter of all things respectable (or so I thought). I edited my profile, as one does when announcing the next move, and christened myself Chief Soul Officer of Soulbbati-cal, with a wink and a smile. Frankly, I assumed it would get lost in the shuffle of legitimate business news and professional accomplish-ments. I was astonished at the torrent of positive—and seemingly envious—reactions that poured in. I hadn't been searching for any sort of external validation of my decision (though I won't deny the serotonin boost), but it made me wonder how many others were harboring unrequited dreams and/or malnourished souls. This was the first moment I began to wonder if this was a calling to share my story to inspire more people to follow their soul's calling.

And what does a former overachiever do after that?

She reverts to what she knows. I began filling my calendar with lunches and dinners and appointments and gym classes and philanthropic board meetings and anything else I could find. I reached out to everyone I knew. Made excuses to buy shit I didn't really need. Finally got to see what the produce aisle of a Whole Foods looks like on a weekday afternoon. Cleaned out my closets. Ran the lakefront trail when it was empty. Enjoyed late lunches where no one cared how long I lingered. And, wandered the Milwaukee Art Museum with so few fellow patrons I could've been naked. (And, believe me, after a little wine at lunch, I was tempted.)

As fun as all of that was, I was defaulting to doing versus being, filling every hour of my day out of fear and habit. Busy-ness is a bitch of an addiction, I discovered. One more thing I would have to conquer on this journey.

The change was wildly unsettling, more so than I expected. As the weeks wore on, there were fewer people with whom to fill my time. I had raised a toast of some sort with nearly everyone I knew in Milwaukee. I was growing incredibly lonely. But it inspired me to embrace the idea of slowing down. I started spending a few afternoons a week reading and writing at the sidewalk café tables at Tre Revali, my favorite Mediterranean restaurant. I was seeking inspiration from Cheryl Strayed's *Wild* and *Brave Enough*, Brené Brown's *The Gifts of Imperfection* and *Daring Greatly*, and Gary Zukav's *The Seat of the Soul*. I was face-to-sun, wine-in-hand, and heart open to what it would take to shift my world forward.

Soon enough, wanderlust kicked in. I dreamt about how reconnecting with distant lands might spark my soul. The only thing that had kept me in Milwaukee was Harley-Davidson.

It was time to move back to Chicago, my springboard to the world. It was time to stop overthinking and overdoing. If I was going to make this work, I had to be willing to shift out of my head and into my soul. It was time to start letting go, trusting the Universe, and surrendering to a deeper inner journey that could take me anywhere.

And boy, did it ever.

9.

IDENTITY CRISIS
(OR, OH FUCK, NOW WHAT DO I DO?)

Moving back to Chicago was like moving on after a breakup. You know the feeling. For at least a handful of months after parting ways, you try to minimize the chances of bumping into your former lover; you avoid stumbling upon people and places that remind you of what was, not wanting to look into a rose-colored rearview mirror and forget the legitimate reasons you said goodbye in the first place. It's too easy. You need space to start fresh, and find the uncoupled version of you again.

That's pretty much how I felt in the beginning. Uncoupled, and a little adrift. In fewer than three months, I had quit Harley, run out the lease on my apartment, sold my killer charcoal-and-white Softail Slim motorcycle, donated thousands of dollars of mint Harley-Davidson merchandise to charities, and resigned from the board of trustees of two Milwaukee-based arts organizations I cherished. The boards were the last to go, because the work had always felt like Soul Fuel to me, rooted in my passion for keeping the arts a vibrant part of our culture. And, truth be told, they kept me busy in the first couple of jobless months. Both organizations asked me to stay on, despite the seats having originally been Harley-Davidson corporate seats, but I knew my next chapter was full-time soul work. I needed to be fully present to myself.

So, I skinnied my life down to the portable essentials: friendships, artwork, and my favorite orange helmet and leather jackets. Oh, and one non-portable essential: my hairstylist (or hair therapist, as I liked to call her). Emily kept my head straight and my locks the perfect shade of rebel red. I was cutting expenses left and right, but signature hair was one element of my identity that I wasn't willing to part with. It felt authentic and on-brand. Whatever the cost, I was shimmying into my Soulbbatical as a rock-star redhead. My courage was wobbly at best in those days, so I was determined to look the part of a badass, even if I didn't feel it.

Moving back into the same loft in Chicago offered some stability and familiarity, but the questions and temptations remained. I had the urge to busy myself with lunches, dinners, happy hours, cultural events, new gym classes, and online wanderlusting. (That's what I call the aimless adventuring down virtual rabbit holes of exotic travel porn. If it was an Olympic sport, I'd be a gold medal contender.) You know what I learned? It's not corporate life itself that makes you busy, it's the art of self-avoidance—doing anything in your power to distract from sitting with your own thoughts and feelings.

Whoever said, "Wherever you go, there you are," nailed it. There I was, with total freedom, and still avoiding quality time with myself. (Shaking my head, as the kids would say.)

At the time, I had no role models for this new and juicy kind of life. I was in the wilderness, alone. Bushwhacking new territory, step by prickly step. Guided by the compass of my newly liberated soul. Knowing only the next right step, never the ultimate destination. Trusting in the prophetic words of Joseph Campbell, "If the path before you is clear, you're probably on someone else's." For the first time in my life, I was truly pioneering my own way forward, and hoping it might intersect with others on a similar journey.

In those early days I would have an "Oh fuck, now what do I do?" moment at least a few times a week. The kind that makes you want to curl up in the fetal position and suck your thumb, abandon your courageous quest for even the briefest taste of the known. I was so used to driving someone else's agenda, I had literally forgotten how to steward my own. What does a people-pleaser do when she has no people left to please? Does she finally please herself?

It felt like a modern-day Zen koan worthy of some reflection. If only I would sit still for a minute.

Forging my own path was more challenging than I expected. I was disappointed to hear people say things like "I wish I was single with no kids so I could do the same thing," or "it must be nice to have the money to not work for a year," or "maybe Harley-Davidson just wasn't the right fit for you."

As if leaving behind a hefty six-figure salary with no one else to pay my mortgage or put food on my table was a no-brainer. As if the decision didn't require ruthless prioritization to make it a reality. It wasn't a luxury afforded me. It was a very intentional choice to turn in the direction of my dreams. One that I believe I would have made under any circumstances—husband, kids, farm animals, you name it. It felt elemental to my existence. Perhaps it seemed fascinating to those around me who fantasized about this very idea every Sunday night. The same folks who always found a "yeah, but . . ." (or five) to justify staying on the treadmill.

How could others possibly understand? And why wouldn't they be envious of my declaration of independence from the fear and self-doubt, and Shackles of Should, that bind so many of us?

It took me twenty-six years on someone else's path before I grew a pair of cojones monstrous enough to impregnate my soul with the courage it would take to venture into the wilderness to discover the meaning of my own life. To make real sacrifices in pursuit of the very thing that eludes so many of us and keeps us trapped in the vicious cycle of desiring more money, indulgences, and shiny objects to fill the gaping void of I'm-not-enough-ness and lack-of-joy-itis. Both are chronic illnesses that can only be cured by looking inward.

So brace yourself, because you'll be tested at every turn on your soul journey. Joseph Campbell and Yoda both knew this about going into the proverbial cave. You have to do it alone, and be willing to face your fears. You have to go through the darkness in order to find the light. This is the part that's often called "the messy middle"— where you question everything, break down often, and pray to whatever higher power you believe in that your XXL cojones will drop quickly.

It's also the bit where massive growth happens—if you let it.

I realized that I had never done messy very well, publicly or privately. I had always kept the mess buried deep, because I thought not having my shit together was a sign of weakness. I was raised to "look on the bright side," "stay strong," and "figure it the fuck out" (FITFO for those in the know). Those mantras had served me well in the corporate world. They kept me in constant motion, anxious to find answers and solve problems, all while sharpening my skills as a ninja of numbing. Stealthily assassinating my own feelings with food and booze as soon as they would appear. Keeping the mess at bay (or so I thought).

One of my first lessons was to embrace the mess. It was time to get comfortable with dropping into my own feelings and asking myself powerful questions. What do I believe in? What scares me? What lights me up? What are my unique gifts? What do I really, really want in this lifetime? It's true that the only way out is through—through the darkness, through the fear, through the uncertainty.

And the only way through is to feel.

I gave myself permission to sit still, be scared, and not try to prove anything to anyone. So much of my identity had been tethered to the thoughts and opinions of others. The Why-dentity in me craved validation for her choices and accomplishments, and the rebel pushed us just far enough off the beaten path. I finally accepted that it wasn't my responsibility to help others feel comfortable with my journey, not even my own family. They would get there on their own—or not.

You may remember that my mom used to say a prayer every night during the teenage hellion years: "Please, God, let me channel this child to adulthood, and let us both be alive when she gets there." I wondered what she was thinking now. Was she working on an update to God? For shits and giggles, I imagined what that might sound like: "Please, God, channel this adult child to sanity and let her not be living in a discarded refrigerator box when she gets there." Or maybe she finally let go of all the formality, grabbed a glass of wine, and just went for the straight woman-to-woman talk: "Hey God, um, yeah, Shelley's going rogue again. I thought we got through the worst of the rebel stuff decades ago. Excuse my language, but I think my daughter has gone bat shit crazy. She's really talented, if a little impulsive. Mike and I have to let her do her thing (again) and just pray she doesn't face-plant in these precious years before retirement. I know she doesn't have the best track record in the church, but I'm wondering if you might keep a closer watch over her until she gets back on track? Thank you and Amen."

Pour, sip, repeat.

My parents might've been the only ones praying for me, but they weren't the only people in my world raising a curious brow. There was a lot of support on the surface—phone calls and texts and an outpouring of love-cum-envy on social media—but I suspect most folks were grabbing the jumbo popcorn, ready to watch events unfold, frame by frame. They wanted to cheer me on but weren't entirely sure whether this cinematic feature would be more *Eat Pray Love* or *The Girl on the Train.* Light or dark. Inspiring or cautionary. Happily ever after—or really, really not.

Of course, I had no clue how this movie would end either. But conviction was my currency, and I was going for broke.

Most days anyway.

Nowhere to Hide

The problem was, I had left behind the only identity I had ever really known. I wasn't Sheryl Sandberg or Bozoma (Boz) Saint John or any other number of celebrity executives with a reputation that transcended the brands they served. I was the smart, passionate, and humble servant who made shit happen. I had never wanted the spotlight. I did my rebel thing behind the scenes, and was rewarded handsomely for it. I had been hiding in corporate culture, and behind big brands, for decades. I had forgotten how to be Shelley Paxton. It was tough to swallow the horse tranquilizer of truth: I was sought after for *what* I was, not necessarily for *who* I was.

I wasn't even sure who Shelley Paxton was anymore under the weighty collection of masks and armor. I was a stranger to myself. With nowhere to hide, I was eyeball-to-hairy-eyeball with my own demons without the crutch of a big job for the first time in my life. Faced with the messy work of chipping away the caked-on layers of crap from the pristine diamond of my soul.

It was time to get clear on my real values and purpose. To believe that *I* am the most valuable and iconic brand I could ever represent. And to not only remind myself that I am a diamond but that I create diamonds in this world. I don't need titles, corporate pressure, and the borrowed equity of other brands. I can do it on my own. Because operating from a place of truth is a kind of superpower. It's the rocket fuel that allows us to play big. That forces us to no longer lurk in the shadows of our own bullshit. So powerful we have no choice but to step out onto the stage and share our humanity and gifts with the world, in the way only we can.

And keep making that choice every day. Despite the fear and doubts.

Believe me, we all have those days (or weeks or months) where we forget our unique and powerful gifts. I've had many—and still do. So, just in case, I have this little love note scrawled in lipstick on my bathroom mirror: "I create fucking diamonds." It's my true north. And it feels more badass than a bumper sticker.

Point of No Return

There's a reason more people don't take this leap. It not only requires courage, it demands commitment. The work is real and the temptations along the way plentiful. The Universe is a beguiling temptress—she'll test your will at every turn. Until you prove your resolve, again and again. You'll be tempted to believe what others are saying, tempted to follow your ego, tempted to throw in the towel and turn back to what you know. I can tell you that it gets easier because it takes so much less effort to show up as your authentic self every day. Notice I said easier, not easy. If you're shooting for the stars, it's never easy, but it is rewarding as hell.

Every fiber of my being was challenged to stay on course. I watched my successor at Harley thrive in her new role, as the congratulatory calls from friends and former colleagues slowed to a trickle. I would become yesterday's news before I could create tomorrow's headlines. Flying in the darkness of potential, before the dawn of becoming. Slowly learning to trust the instrument panel of my soul.

For the first handful of months, my phone vibrated with demands from prestigious executive recruitment firms. They were dangling opportunities to jump into even bigger chief marketing officer roles, at companies with mega-brands and massive budgets. Exponentially larger than what we had ever played with at Harley. And then there was that well-funded technology start-up and one of the fastest growing online travel brands. I wasn't really interested in any of them, but I was curious. Correction: My ego was curious, and terrified of closing the corporate door for good. Apparently, my ego was still flying the plane.

So I did the awkward dance. Entertaining conversations for the sake of someone else's plan B. Attempting to quiet the cautionary chorus in my head: *What if everyone is right to be concerned? What if this exploration doesn't work out? Will anyone even be willing to talk to me after a year off the radar?* It felt shitty and insincere—like having a backup date to the prom just in case your long-shot true love doesn't pan out. Old habits sure do die hard AF.

I even took a few lunches at Soho House Chicago with well-known recruiters. I might've been hedging my bets, but I was doing it on my terms. Even as they spoke, I was clear about my intention to be out of the market for at least a year. I tried to help the powers that be understand why I was doing what I was doing, and how I hoped to start a trend of leaders who would blaze trails from productivity to possibility, say yes to being as much as doing, and start rewriting the script of success. Though I wasn't entirely sure what that looked like yet.

And then the phone calls stopped. Not only from recruiters but also from old colleagues. From the only network I'd ever known. Business acquaintances I'd mistaken for friends. I was no longer a conduit to brands everyone wanted a piece of. I had become a straight-up enigma.

Redefining Rebel

Maybe a rebel enigma, if there is such a thing. The beauty of this journey is that you can invent things—words, titles, jobs, whatever works for you. Create it and own it like the badass you are. That's what I did, and it worked out pretty damn well (if I do say so myself).

But, I'm not gonna lie. Redefining what it meant to be a rebel—and learning to harness this energy in a new way—was tricky at first. I was no longer rebelling *against* tradition or corporate norms or the status quo, as I had been for my entire existence. I wasn't seeking to define myself against others' journeys or traditional status. I was learning to rebel *for* my own life, *for* my own fulfillment, *for* my own path forward. I was discovering the rebel truth: that authenticity is the truest form of rebellion.

Soulbbatical is the conscious choice to explore the truth and purpose of who you are. It's the process of shedding any identities that take you out of alignment with your authentic self. It's about embracing vulnerability and receptivity, the modalities of the soul. And it invites you into a life of ease and grace (versus struggle and strife). As part of this journey, I've learned that the real power of rebellion comes *from* a place of passion and conviction. As I said earlier, the world needs more of us rebelling *for* what we believe in, and doing it in a way that is 100 percent true to who we are (not who we think we should be or how we think we should look).

Perhaps this is what Theodore Roosevelt meant by the (wo)man in the arena. I was finally daring to show up and be seen. But, first I needed to lay down my armor, piece by shiny piece. Until I was as naked and vulnerable as the day I was born. (Although, let's be real, the flesh rolls and negative thigh gap looked a hell of a lot cuter back then.)

From Productivity to Possibility

How do we get so armored up in the first place? Well, we learn to be warriors, to protect and deflect, especially when our internal boundaries have eroded over time. Layers of armor can become like the hundreds of apps on our smartphones—seemingly helpful on the surface, but ultimately destructive in the behaviors they drive. Imagine if we could restore ourselves to factory settings—our raw gifts and talents and potential; our most authentic selves sans armor. What is preventing us from connecting on the deepest levels possible with others and the world? Is it the apps and games and social norms that have conditioned us to always be on, hustling for status and doubting our own worth? Could we just stop the numbing and distraction? Could we embrace stillness and our truest desires? Could we create space for meaning, synchronicity, and what matters most? Could we shift from lives of obsessive productivity to ones of infinite possibility? I started to wonder what it could look like to put this into practice.

As the external gratification faded away, I had no choice but to focus my attention inward and to remind myself why I was doing this in the first place, especially after one too many conversations like this:

A well-meaning friend: So what exactly are you going to *do*?

Me: It may sound crazy, but I have no agenda other than to nourish my soul and reconnect with myself and those I love. I'm letting it unfold organically.

Him: That sounds like a lot of Netflix and happy hours. I'm envious. Seriously, I mean, what do you do all day?

Me: Funny, it's not about *doing* at all. It's about simply being with myself, asking some tough questions, and seeing where it takes me.

That well-meaning friend, now utterly confused: Hmmmmm. Interesting.

The word "interesting" has always been my go-to when I literally have no idea what else to say. I assume it was the same for him. The clear subtext was "are you sure you know what you're doing?"

It was enough to motivate me to remind myself how I really wanted to show up for myself on Soulbbatical. So, I wrote a little love note in my journal:

I want to . . .

- Create space, health, creativity, connection, movement
- Reclaim my mornings—morning time is me time, journaling, meditation, exercise, creation, all relaxed not rushed
- Be present—don't worry about the past or fret about the future; what will be will be
- Learn to sit in stillness—engage with myself and my scared-shitlessness rather than doing everything possible to avoid me/it
- Listen to my soul—what does it need? What does it want? Where does it want to take me?
- Rediscover my unique gifts
- Get clear on my values
- Get outside (a lot)
- Reconnect with friends and family
- Seek inspiration on what it looks like to live differently— read *Thrive*, *The 4-Hour Workweek*, *Tools of Titans*, *Man's Search for Meaning*, Brené Brown everything
- Change up my environment—break the routine of doing, get inspired, start writing and photography again
- Leave space for creativity, synchronicity and serendipity. Opportunity to wander and wonder

After sitting with that list for a while, letting it sink into my consciousness, two things became crystal clear to me:

My highest values are freedom, courage, authenticity, and connection. They always have been. Hell, I'm an Enneagram 7—the enthusiastic visionary, epicurean, and adventurer—and a borderline introvert who appreciates intimate experiences and deep connections. I'm easily bored by the mundane and exhausted by the superficial. It's no wonder that, without boundaries of steel in place, corporate life—even when it involved riding motorcycles around the world—took its toll on me.

It was time for a change of scenery. Not only to signal a reboot to my brain but also to lean into my values. Travel budgets had all but disappeared in my last two years at Harley, so I suddenly realized that my soul was craving freedom and new experiences. Perhaps that's where I would reconnect with myself and create my new reality.

As if the Universe was peering over my shoulder and peeking at my journal (oh, who am I kidding? Of course she was!), two days later I got a note from an old friend who I hadn't spoken to in years. Shari, a former marketer turned entrepreneur and hospitality maven, had moved with her husband and two young kids to an idyllic village in southwest France. What started as a search for a holiday home near the beaches of La Rochelle had become a labor of love to renovate a quintessential white stone French château into a luxe bed and breakfast and permanent family home. She invited me to begin my Soulbbatical at Manoir du Moulin, so I could experience the slow, beautiful roll of rural life, home cooking, and people living out their soul's purpose, every day.

Synchronicity at its finest.

I was a "Hell yes." It was time to get this show on the road.

Soul Search

CouRaGe

1. On a scale from 1 to 10, how courageously are you living your life right now?

   > 1 = I'm shackled in Shouldville
   > 10 = I put the capital "B" in Bravery and Badass
   >
   > 1 2 3 4 5 6 7 8 9 10
   >
   > Don't even think about checking 7. It's a cop-out, a safe place to hide. Be courageous enough to push yourself to the 6 or the 8, as Tim Ferriss would say.

2. What would you do if you knew you had:

   Less time:_____

   More money:_____

   No chance of failing:_____

3. Where might you be fighting for your limitations instead of your possibilities? Imagine that you've stopped shuffling through your usual deck of excuses (time, money, fear of failure) for a moment; how might that reveal a clean slate to make some big shifts happen?

4. Where are you pretending to have your shit together?

5. What in your life is sucking you dry, and where's the fuel you know would ignite your energy? (Reflect back on the Soul Fuel vs Soul Sucks exercise on pages 133–34 for inspiration.) What do you need to say *no* to in order to say *yes* to what matters most to you?

6. Where do you find yourself doing what you feel you *should* do instead of what you *want* to do? If you had all the courage you believe you need, what would change? If you get to the end of your life and haven't created these things, how will you feel?

S.O.U.L. Process

After spending time reflecting on the questions above, choose one new insight or truth you want to take action on now and follow the S.O.U.L. process below. Use this for as many insights as you want. Lather, rinse, repeat.

S: **Show up.** Commit to having integrity with yourself. Stop hiding and playing safe. State aloud the new truth you want to create in service of your authentic self. (It often starts with "I am_____," "I will_____," or "I can_____.")

O: **Own it.** Repeat the truth until you believe it's possible, and then accept responsibility for making it happen. Evict any competing stories and disempowering language (I can't/I should/I have to) from your mind.

U: **Unleash it.** Put clear intentions into the Universe. Share your truth with those who will support, inspire, and/or mentor you. Take one small step toward what you want to create, and witness the synchronicity that follows. The Universe opens one door at a time.

L: **Live it.** Create boundaries and make conscious choices in service of your new truth. Prioritize it. Get creative. Ditch the excuses. Live the idea of who you want to become, or what you want to create, *before you're ready.*

Section 4:

Purpose

10.

ZEN AND THE ART OF MOTORCYCLE PHILOSOPHY

Fall in France—Letting Go, Slowing Down

Shari's invitation was only the beginning of the serendipity that would shape my Soulbbatical. I didn't always know why I was called to a certain place, but I quickly learned to trust that the lessons would be revealed soon enough.

Three weeks and three flights after we reconnected, I landed in the city of Nantes, rented a car, and drove south toward the popular port of La Rochelle. My half-mast eyes caught the marker for the blink-and-you'll-miss-it sign for the bucolic little village of Sainte-Hermine just in time to make the turn. A precariously narrow cobbled main street ushered me into the sleepy center of town. Sun-bleached white stone buildings with terra-cotta-tiled roofs lined the streets. I counted exactly two restaurants, a bakery, a farmers' market, a butcher, a pub, a cinema, a school, a church, and a post office. I mean, what else does one need, really? Wine, of course, but there's no shortage of that in France, and Bordeaux was only a two-and-a-half-hour drive away. I was already starting to relax.

The village streets were quiet. Summer tourists had gone, and the usual laissez-faire pace of life had resumed. A few locals sauntered about in the nonchalant way of the French, where no one looks to be in a hurry or stressed about their impossibly long to-do list. It didn't take me long to figure out that this chapter was going to be about slowing waaaaaay down, and embracing the simple pleasures. Shari was in cahoots with the Universe. As a former executive herself, she knew exactly what my soul needed.

Entering the gates of Manoir du Moulin was like a soul-gasm—mind, body, and spirit swelling in response to the stunning beauty of the château, the scent of rosemary in the fall breeze, the warm sun on my face, the sound of tranquility, and the welcome taste of the chilled Côtes de Provence Rosé that Shari handed me upon arrival. I immediately felt more present, more feminine, and softer around the edges. (Just like I do after a particularly spectacular orgasm!) The French sure have the seduction thing nailed. I wondered if there was such a thing as soul-duction? Had I just experienced it? If so, I wanted more.

The next twelve days were everything I never knew I needed, and then some. Of course I had known it was time to bust out of the busy-ness, but I'd had no clue how or where to start. I wasn't even sure what slow looked like, outside of meditation and sleep and service in the Caribbean islands.

But in Sainte-Hermine, life moved at the pace of the sun itself. Each day brought fresh croissants, tomatoes off the vine, and eggs delivered in a basket straight from the source. Home-cooked meals were sacred, and the time we spent connecting over them, even more so. The art of living in the present was being modeled all around me. Daily life was a bountiful gift to be savored, not an epic struggle to be tolerated. I realized that it wasn't just my college French that was rusty; so was my language of being. It was time for a full-on cultural immersion.

Au revoir to the culture of cortisol. No more speeding in the thirty-five-miles-per-hour zone of life.

Each day was a new opportunity for discovery and connection with Shari and her family. We picked fresh fruit, veggies, and herbs from their massive garden every day, then strolled around town with our market bags to find other ingredients that complemented our harvest. What fresh cuts did the butcher have in stock? What kind of bread had the bakery made that morning? What cheeses and other goodies were available at the farmers' market? I loved these questions, because they didn't presume any one right answer. It was one big epicurean treasure hunt designed by the Universe. And the bounty never failed to inspire.

Shari cooked nearly every meal from scratch, while I looked on in wide-eyed wonder, diligently keeping our wine glasses topped off. This time together around the dinner table, in the garden, in front of the fireplace, with Shari, Warren, their kids, and a few other off-season guests, yielded a deep, visceral sense of connectedness that I hadn't even realized was missing in my life. One that had presumably been cockblocked by all the technology and armor and, well, that busy-ness thing I did so well. Slowing down was already helping me drop deeper into experiences and relationships. Conversations became provocative, not pedantic, because we weren't also texting or taking calls or worrying about the future. We were savoring the present—as the gift it was meant to be.

Pretty soon I settled deeper into a connection with myself. I gave myself permission to take a bath for the first time in years. I was always the "power shower" girl, because it was quick and efficient. But now there just happened to be an inviting Japanese soaking tub in my guest room. (Thank you, Shari.) In case you're wondering, I highly recommend it with darkness and candles and beautiful silence. A silky glass of Bordeaux doesn't hurt either.

Warning: It may become a habit. Soaking in the tub turned out to be my gateway drug to the power of stillness. I started craving the opportunity to sit still and tune in. Shari and the kids would frequently find me perched on a chaise longue in the garden. No book, no journal, no checklist of sightseeing opportunities, just being with my thoughts and feelings and emotions. Noticing what was present—bliss (*I've never felt so relaxed and connected*), gratitude (*I'm so thankful for this experience*), curiosity (*Can people really live their lives this way all the time? Can I?*), uncertainty (*Where is this all leading? And what's next?*), and of course, fear (*What if I have to go back to my old lifestyle when this year is over?*).

I was choosing Human Being over Human Doing.

One of the memories-cum-lessons that brought it all into focus for me was my first bike ride with Shari's seven-year-old son, Jacobi. He's an old soul bursting with young energy. Outside of school, you could pretty much always find him imagining elaborate dinner parties in the garden, entertaining guests of the B&B with his dance moves, cartwheeling his way across the backyard, or doing double backflips on the trampoline. He also loved to ride his bike into the countryside. It was refreshing to see kids in the wild again, creating their own fun, not slaves to a screen. Kind of like those of us who grew up back in the middle ages, with analog everything.

On the first Saturday after breakfast, Jacobi asked Shari if he could take me on a bike ride, just the two of us. I loved the idea, not only because this precocious little ginger had already stolen my heart, but also because I was desperate for some exercise. A steady diet of the OG superfoods—wine, bread, cheese, meat, and olives—was threatening to slingshot the top button of my jeans into the eye of an innocent bystander. Shari didn't miss a beat in saying yes. She trusted her kid and knew it would be an adventure for me.

Within minutes, we were in the garage gearing up. Before I could even get our water bottles into the saddlebags of the three-speed cruiser, Jacobi took off like a bull out of a chute. His mini mountain bike kicked up a cloud of dust as he powered through the gravel toward the front gate, screaming, "C'mon, Shelley! Let's go!" I looked back at Shari for any words of advice, but she just waved and shouted, "Have fun, kids!" I scrambled to catch up with Jacobi and, just like that, we were off. We pedaled through a park, up a hill, past more quaint stone homes, across miles of open fields, under a viaduct, and off the beaten path through some dense trees. We'd been riding for well over an hour when suddenly Jacobi stopped. He looked perplexed.

"Do you know where we are?" I asked, dreading the answer.

"Yes," he replied confidently. "I want to show you this cute little babbling brook with a bridge, and I thought it was here. I think we have to go a bit farther into the woods."

"Have you been there before? Are you sure this is the right way?"

"I found it with my dad one time. You'll love it. We can put our feet in the water." He was so excited to share his discovery with me. I couldn't bring myself to tell him I was worried this magical brook might not actually exist. The urban cynic in me was already envisioning the headline: "American Executive Loses Self and Local Child in Vain Search for Soul." My inner control freak, on orange alert, besieged my brain with pleas to call this kids' bluff and turn back before we became dinner for French wolves. (Not that we had seen one. For all I knew, they were as imaginary as the babbling brook we were seeking.)

Admittedly, my sense of direction is less than stellar. I'm the type who gets lost on a city grid. I respond with a blank stare if someone gives me directions that involve the words "north, south, east, west." I may as well be trying to find the Big Dipper in daylight. So I knew I wouldn't be the one getting us back to Manoir du Moulin if we were, in fact, lost.

But this was Jacobi's backyard. His playground. It was my invitation from the Universe to trust and surrender. And to learn French children's songs from an adventurous Canadian ginger in the blissful middle of nowhere. You can't script these moments.

And sure enough, after another twenty or thirty minutes of riding, we heard water. There it was: a picturesque little bridge and brook, just as Jacobi had promised. We jumped off our bikes, high-fived each other, and let our toes mingle in the water with the tadpoles and the frogs.

I was literally being a kid. Letting go. And it felt amazing.

We played on the rocks for ages. I lost track of time. It didn't matter. I trusted that we were in the exact right place, doing exactly what we were supposed to be doing. And that Jacobi instinctively knew his way home. We had plenty of hours of sunlight still to enjoy.

I chuckled as I imagined a conversation in my head:

Me: *What's the worst than can happen?*
Myself: *The adventure continues.*
I: *Exactly.* (Hat tip to the Universe.)

Not only did we make it back to Manoir du Moulin with no problem, we went on two more biking expeditions while I was there.

Each time a new route, a new discovery, a new adventure. I was leaning hard into these priceless reminders to let go, slow down, and embrace my inner child more often.

I knew the challenge would be to keep practicing this new way of being when I got home. Somewhere over the Atlantic, on my return flight, I reflected on how even my language was shifting to softer, kinder, more inviting, and less rushed. I felt less compelled to fill a silence. The most common phrase in my vocabulary for decades, "I'm crazy busy," was gone. It had been my default response because it was true. I wore it like a badge of honor. It fed my worthiness—and my avoidance. (Ego: 2, Soul: 0.) With France fresh in my mind, I penned a commitment to myself in my journal:

If you ever catch yourself saying crazy busy *again, stop immediately and figure out what you are doing wrong and why. Let your soul set the pace from now on. Screw the clock.*

Winter in New Zealand—The Inner Work

My experience in Sainte-Hermine reminded me of the words celebrated by motorcyclists everywhere: "Life is a journey, not a destination." The phrase is a powerful reminder to slow down, take the scenic route, and be present to all the things you would miss out on if you took the straight and narrow (and oh-so-boring) highway at high speed. Create the space and savor the moments along the way—the unexpected beauty, people, ideas, and opportunities the Universe will drop in your path.

It suddenly dawned on me that my mind-set was mashing up with my motorcycle roots. I was being reminded of critical truths that I had learned on the bike, but hadn't considered how they might play out in everyday life. Not only the possibility of savoring the journey but also the power of being present. There's no such thing as multitasking on a motorcycle; distraction is disaster. Why do we think we can be so good at it anywhere else?

Total face palm moment. Did it take walking away from Harley to reveal lessons that had been there all along?

That aha led me back to one of my favorite books of all time, *Zen and the Art of Motorcycle Maintenance: An Inquiry into Values* by Robert M. Pirsig. On the surface, it's a story about a father and son taking a summer motorcycle trip across the American Northwest in the 1970s. Through the metaphor of motorcycle maintenance, it reveals a much more profound philosophical exploration of how we live, and how we can live better. The result is a deeply personal journey of discovery, growth, love, and acceptance. A real self-reckoning.

I was reading through the lens of my soul this time around and feeling a powerful connection to Pirsig over three decades later. Was I now on a similar journey of self-exploration, only off the bike and in foreign lands? Was Soulbbatical becoming *Zen and the Art of Motorcycle Philosophy: An Inquiry into Soulful Living*? A twenty-first century exploration of what it means to live better?

That idea got me fired up.

I felt an unquenchable desire to find a spirit land that would inspire me to go deeper. Someplace remote and wild where I could learn to love me until I was me again. Someplace I had never been. Bali was too predictable for my rebel soul—it's where everyone goes to find his or her spiritual self and this wasn't an *Eat, Pray, Love* journey (as much as I adored that book and everything Liz Gilbert).

I wasn't sure where my soul compass would lead me, when serendipity intervened again. I got a message from my friend Torie, a New Zealander living in Hong Kong who I lovingly refer to as Doleeza (long story). We had worked in the ad business together before I left for Harley, but we hadn't spent quality time together in years. She had seen the news about my Soulbbatical on social media and was reaching out to give me a proper Kiwi "Good on ya!" (English translation: "Well done! Congrats!") I told her about France and that I was seeking my next soul-scape.

She didn't even give me a chance to finish my sentence. My little iMessage bubbles were still percolating when she launched in with: "New Zealand is your place, girl. Not just because it's my homeland. It's extraordinarily beautiful and layered with the rich culture of the Maori. You'll find so much inspiration there—in the water, the mountains, the people, the tramps, the wines. That last one in particular knowing you . . ." (laugh emoji, laugh emoji, laugh emoji).

"I'm more interested in learning why tramps may be inspiring. Are you suggesting I need to get laid?" I shot back, chuckling to myself. Maybe I did need a little *Eat, Pray, Love*'n.

"LOL. Tramping is hiking in New Zealand. Our hiking trails are world-class. Gorgeous places for you to do your soul-searching thing. And maybe you'll get laid too!" (More laugh emojis).

Boom. Everything I was looking for on the other side (or under side?) of the world. New Zealand was high on the bucket list for me, but it wasn't your typical one-to-two-week holiday destination. It demanded at least three weeks to really experience both islands. When else would I be free for three weeks or more?

If not now, when?

I announced my decision on the socials the very next day. I would be going to New Zealand in January to escape the Chicago winter and warm my soul in the summer prime of the southern hemisphere. I asked for recommendations from friends and family, and a few Kiwi friends scattered across the planet. As thoughts started to pour in, my phone rang. It was my friend Kerri in San Francisco, a rock-star marketing executive in between jobs and also looking for some soul time. She asked if I was open to having a partner-in-crime on the trip. The craziest bit is that we were originally introduced through our mutual friend Brent, a native Kiwi. Talk about synchronicity. You just can't make this shit up.

Two months later (and, not coincidentally, only days after the Trump inauguration) we landed in Auckland to start our three-week adventure, soon to be christened "Climbs & Vines." We tramped spectacular trails from Queen Charlotte to Abel Tasman to Roys Peak, and rewarded ourselves with the nectar of the gods in the glorious wine regions of Hawke's Bay, Marlborough, and Central Otago. A helicopter dropped us onto blue glaciers and the beaches of remote mountain lakes. Ferries carried us across the Cook Strait and through the waterfalls of Milford Sound. The scenery zinged a current through my body, the likes of which I'd never experienced. I'd traveled to more than sixty countries in my lifetime, but never had I felt so energized, and so at home. I could write a *War and Peace*–length love note to New Zealand. An entire novel about how the experience transformed me as a human. But we don't have eight hundred pages, so let me summarize it this way: Kerri left after three weeks. I didn't.

Actually, my soul wouldn't let me. I had more work to do on my own. And I knew this was the place to do it. I had found my spirit land. So I rescheduled my flight, rebooked the rental car, and started my solo journey from the South Island back to the North Island in search of a little seaside cottage where I could be alone and begin to peel back the layers. A friend recommended that I make my way up to the Bay of Islands, north of Auckland, to start my search for the perfect *bach* (Kiwi to English translation: "cottage"). The old me would have jumped on a plane from Queenstown to Auckland pronto. The new me wanted to slow down and savor the journey. The new me realized that that's where the real work would begin.

The outer journey took me over the mountains and up the rugged west coast before stopping in Golden Bay, on the northwestern tip of the South Island. Straight to a little family-run, five-cottage resort appropriately named Adrift. The Universe had led me to exactly where I was supposed to be—hands off the wheel, floating in the sea of self-reflection.

The next morning I picked up my laptop and began to write. I was finally ready to experience and embrace the creativity that I had boxed into PowerPoint for so many years. I've always loved writing, and yet I didn't pursue it outside of my job. I didn't blog or write articles or allow myself to even play with the possibility. I can't explain why, beyond a raw admission that I was scared—and constantly questioning my own credibility and voice. Even with a big job, I was playing small at life.

But now the creative spigot was starting to flow. I found these words channeling from my soul through my fingertips: "I love writing prose. What's kept me from it all these years? Why have I felt so blocked from my own thoughts and ideas? Perhaps true creativity only happens when you let go. When you drop the armor and the expectations and the judgment. When you quit the struggle. When you're willing to open your heart and listen to your soul. When you're brave enough to face what's ready to come out. When fear becomes fuel instead of resistance. Only then will the kinks in the hose be released. And words will flow free."

And they did. A little more each day.

By the time I made it up to Auckland, I realized I was liberating my soul from the clutches of my ego. It was a daily ~~battle~~ practice to lean into the discomfort and uncertainty. And there's another motorcycle truth: the simple fact is that motorcycles turn by our leaning into them. The rider pushes down on the handlebar in the direction of the turn and leans into it in order to guide the bike in "cornering" the turn. If you waver, you'll wobble, or even stall, mid-turn. The art is to lean in, roll on the throttle, and fully commit. When you first learn this principle, it feels counterintuitive and scary. You're convinced that the bike is going to tip over and pin you to the ground, but if you don't lean in, you'll end up veering out of your lane or possibly off the road. And, as you may guess, that doesn't end well.

Here I was, on the other side of the planet, realizing that leaning into a turn is the equivalent of leaning into an opportunity in life. Being all in and committed to momentum in the direction you're headed, however terrifying it may feel in that moment. Don't fucking wobble, I reminded myself.

But, for once, I didn't need a reminder. I was leaning so hard into this journey my knee was practically scraping the ground. It was day thirty-two of a nineteen-day trip, and I wasn't stopping. So I posted this open letter to my parents on Facebook:

Dear Mom and Dad,

I know I've been gone a while, but I'm alive and well. Actually the most vibrant kind of alive and deeply soulful kind of well I've felt in a long time. If I didn't know better I'd swear there was a kiwi nesting at the base of our family tree. I feel a sense of freedom and a kindred spirit here that has inspired and focused me in ways I couldn't have imagined. And I'm finally

writing, from an open mind and heart, with a liberating lack
of fear and self-consciousness.

So . . . I've decided to hang around these magical islands
a little while longer to see what else they stir up in this old
soul of mine. I found a little seaside bach up in the Bay of
Islands where I can settle in with my laptop and a view.

Don't worry, I will eventually come home. Increasingly
gray roots and a dwindling supply of contact lenses will
force my hand by mid-March. After four flight changes
(and counting), United Airlines may be more surprised than
anyone when I actually show up for a scheduled departure.

Since Kerri is no longer here to cajole me into selfies,
I've posted a picture as proof of my wellness and desperate
side part attempt to keep the grays hidden. Good thing I'm
traveling with three hats!

I'll see you for Easter in Naples. Love you both
very much. Thank you for raising me to be confident,
independent, headstrong, courageous, and curious (though I
know I've made you regret it on more than one occasion!).

Your Irish-Kiwi-Crazy Daughter,
Shel

With that I rented another car and left Auckland for the four-
hour journey north. After a week in a cute cottage that turned out
to be more sea*view* than sea*side*, I stumbled upon the cottage of
my dreams online and negotiated three weeks for a steal. It was the
end of high season, and the owners loved the concept of Soulbbatical. They were kindred spirits from the UK who had sailed around
the world together, fell in love with New Zealand, and never left.

Within days, I changed my flight (again) and moved to Reef Cottage on pristine Maori land outside of Kerikeri. It was the quintessential shabby chic, sand-in-your-toes, waves-practically-lapping-at-your-doorstep kind of place, on the serene shores of Tapuaetahi Beach.

Well, serene most of the time. The day I showed up, a rare and epic monsoon had descended upon the region. Seriously, I'm talking torrential sideways rain, and the threat of the Pacific Ocean inviting itself into the living room at any minute. I didn't see any host instructions on what to do in that case. Higher ground was an open pasture with cows and no shelter—or my kitchen counter with a bottle of wine and a prayer.

The stunning weather I had experienced (and raved about to friends) for weeks disappeared in a nanosecond. Mother Nature was pissed off. And so was I. Gone were my plans to hike and walk and swim and write on the open-air front porch without getting drenched (or electrocuted). I was starting to wobble. Then it hit me—this is *exactly* the kind of resistance that gets served up when you're at a critical emotional juncture. Was I going to own the situation, or let it own me? Was I going to lean into the challenge, or let it squash what I came here to do?

I chose to hunker down . . . with myself. No more running, hiding, avoiding, drinking. The Universe had me under house arrest. It was time to do the hard work. I hadn't traveled here with a back-breaking arsenal of personal-development books for nothing: *The Untethered Soul, Man's Search for Meaning, The War of Art, The Big Leap, The Dark Side of the Light Chasers, You Are a Badass,* and *Tools of Titans.* I was officially transitioning from getting lost in award-winning fiction to getting found in life-reclaiming nonfiction, aka personal development. I was late to the party, and had a lot of catching up to do.

For the next five tempestuous and very sober days, I stayed put with my demons and my desires—sitting, screaming, crying, listening, writing, resisting, questioning, meditating, and ultimately surrendering to what I knew in my soul to be true. I was still mourning the loss of the identity that had defined me for twenty-six years. My biggest fear was becoming irrelevant and fading into the shadows. Getting summarily deleted from thousands of contact lists around the world because I wasn't tethered to something of greater value. I imagined a chart of my own professional value plummeting like the Dow in 2008. Would it flatline or rebound? I drew an ellipsis . . . and a giant question mark.

Suddenly I was possessed to scrawl, viciously and almost illegibly, the same sentence over and over like Bart Simpson on his homeroom chalkboard:

Who the fuck am I? Who the fuck am I? Who the fuck am I? Who the fuck am I? Who the fuck am I? Who the fuck am I? Who the fuck am I? WHO THE FUCK...

Hold the phone. Epiphany on line 1. I am *who* I am, not *what* I do. I would always have my achievements. No one could take those from me. And I didn't need titles or big brands or a partner to make me worthy, or lovable, or whole. I needed my own love and kindness and compassion. I needed to acknowledge and celebrate my gifts. I needed to believe in me.

I am enough, I wrote below all the questions. And then stared at the words for hours, trying to make sense of the statement.

Perhaps my biggest fear was to show up as my authentic self in the world. To show people the real me. To *face* the real me.

It was time to forgive myself for years of self-hatred and neglect. And start the practice of loving me again. I grabbed my journal and began a stream-of-consciousness scribble about who I am.

I'm not big titles, I'm powerful and innate qualities:

I am beautiful.
I am sexy.
I am soul.
I am soft.
I am funny.
I am love.
I am strength.
I am integrity.
I am courage.
I am bold.
I am brilliant.
I am a badass.
I am a rebel.
I am a role model.
I am a trailblazer.
I am a lighthouse.
I am uniquely and authentically me.
I am living my best life.

The next morning I continued,

I am not the shape of my body.
I am not the titles I held.
I am not the things that I did.
I am not the mistakes that I made.

I am not the appointments on my calendar.

I am not the stories in my head.

I am not the validation or judgment of others.

I am me. And I am enough.

And then my hand gently wrote words I had never uttered in my lifetime: *I love you, Shelley.* I sat in silence, repeating those words, as tears of surrender streamed down my cheeks. I had longed to hear those words from family, friends, partners, bosses, anyone. But never reflected on the power of saying them to myself—or actually believing them.

I practiced saying "I love you, Shelley" in the bathroom mirror. Believe me, it was as awkward and uncomfortable as small talk on a blind date. Sometimes I would stare at myself for ten minutes before I could even muster the words. Sometimes I rolled my eyes and pointed a finger gun at my head. Sometimes I got scared and walked away. But the practice helped me see and appreciate myself for the first time—and even learn to simply smile at myself instead of scowl. And eventually it got easier. (Not just because I was stuck alone in a cottage at the edge of the world in an apocalyptic storm, though I'll admit that might have accelerated things a bit.)

I emerged from the storm with greater purpose. The sun was shining inside and out. In the clear blue skies of my mind, I finally understood that I had an opportunity to change my life and the lives of so many others. It was my time to step out and dare greatly. A chance to bravely model what it looks like to focus on where you want to go, not obsess with what you're trying to avoid.

Imagine that, another motorcycle truth.

One of the first things you learn in motorcycle training: If you fixate on the obstacle in your path, you'll end up hitting it. Guaranteed. You have to fully turn your head (not just your eyes), look where you want to go, and the bike will follow. The key is to make sure you are locked in on the road, not the wall or the tree or the ditch. Otherwise, bad shit happens. Just like in real life. The difference off the bike is that the consequences aren't always as dramatic . . . until they are.

I got more comfortable simply being with myself. Being gentle and kind instead of demanding. Being in conversation with my body and soul. Trusting and listening and learning from what they were trying to tell me. At the cottage, I started a morning routine based on some nuggets I picked up from Tim Ferriss and the A-listers featured in *Tools of Titans*: morning pages (gratitude and journaling), meditation (fifteen to twenty minutes), and movement (kayaking or hiking or swimming). It struck me that I had never been consistent and disciplined about a morning routine, or doing things for myself every day. I would routinely start and stop a new habit within weeks or do it only if I could "squeeze it in" between work obligations. Even my exercise was planned around my work schedule instead of vice versa. It was time to start my days with more intention and compassion and connection. More me-ness.

And then the soul bomb hit: self-first isn't self-ish. It's fundamental. How can we serve others, and have the impact we want in the world, without first making sure that we're healthy and energized? What if the first thing we schedule on our calendars every week is our nonnegotiable me-time? Blocking time for me-tings with ourselves, where we fuel our souls. I scribbled in my journal: *I want a life with more me-tings (Soul Fuels) than meetings (Soul Sucks).*

I felt the impact of a morning routine immediately. Words flooded out of me, as I processed feelings about my relationships, desires, dreams, the decision to leave Harley. My relationship to activity also shifted. I was committed to movement and experiences that fostered and challenged a deeper relationship with myself— reflective walks through the cow pastures, hikes in spiritually significant places, swims and kayaks as far out and as close to the dolphins (my spirit animals) as I could get. Nature was my new conference room, or #church, as Melissa Urban, cofounder of Whole30, calls it. I was a convert.

My final soul-journ in New Zealand was out to Cape Reinga, the northernmost tip of the North Island, and tumultuous point where the Pacific Ocean and the Tasman Sea collide. It's also sacred land, where the Maori believe their spirits leap off into the underworld after dying. Thousands of tourists gawk at the view, visit the famous lighthouse at the point, and drive away with the requisite pictures. My soul was called to venture off the beaten path for miles, with no one else in sight. It felt like an invitation to bury the old me. To let the spirit of Corporate Shelley leap into the great beyond so that Soulful Shelley could emerge, fresh and uncontested. I stood miles from civilization, in the sizzling sun, holding a ceremony for my former self. Loving her for serving me well, and letting her go in honor of the future. I tore a blank page out of my journal and wrote down everything I was ready to release: fear, not-enough-ness, self-loathing, people-pleasing, should-ing, and the unbearably weighty armor associated with maintaining it all. I read the page aloud to the Universe, folded it into the best paper airplane I could, and shot it into the welcoming horizon of the sea-ocean-underworld. It was one of my most powerful experiences in New Zealand. (In case you're wondering, or cursing me for littering, there are more environmentally conscious recommendations in the Soul Search: Purpose section.)

For the record, when Soulful Shelley passes, I want her ashes scattered at Cape Reinga. I'm far too claustrophobic to be buried in a wooden box six feet under and, besides, being tossed to the wind, in a deeply spiritual place, sounds way more Soulbbatical, right? It feels like the ultimate act of authenticity, courage, and purpose.

With that ceremony, I felt complete and ready to say my farewells. The very clever guest book at Reef Cottage was a giant jar of seashells from Tapuaetahi Beach and a collection of Sharpies. I grabbed the extra-large, pearlescent pink shell that my soul sparked to and wrote, "March '17. Absolutely magical. I'll be back . . . Shelley XOXO." That same afternoon, I crossed the threshold onto United Airlines flight 916 from Auckland to San Francisco. I distinctly remember taking a picture of that moment for my sister. Like so many others, she said she wouldn't believe it until she saw it. What I couldn't believe is how much pride I had in looking at the name on my boarding pass, Michelle Elisa Paxton, and thinking, *Now, she's a force to be reckoned with.*

Summer in the Canadian Rockies—Passion and Presence

Okay, so I left New Zealand, but I didn't exactly make it back to Chicago right away. I might have paused for a while in California to reconnect with Kerri, and to take advantage of another moment of serendipity with my long-lost friend Ian down the coast in Avila Beach. Soulful Shelley was definitely at the helm. Oh, she also might have hijacked the rental car and overshot SFO by about two hundred miles in an attempt to tick Lake Tahoe off her bucket list.

Check. In peak rebel form, she would've continued the push east if Avis hadn't threatened to call the police. Spoilsports.

But I did make it to Naples for Easter that year. By the hair of my chinny-chin-chin. It was the last time I saw my dad in his natural, able-bodied, and vibrant state. We laughed and drank and, honestly, probably took it all for granted. Because no one ever thinks it's going to end, right? My parents still wondered where I was headed with this harebrained Soulbbatical idea, and whether I was talking to any recruiters about real job opportunities, but they admitted they could sense a change in my being. They commented that I felt more present and lighthearted, happier than they had seen me in years. We uncorked a bottle of Silver Oak Cabernet Sauvignon and toasted to the (very uncertain) future.

France and New Zealand inspired me to keep rolling. I didn't necessarily *need* to travel to do the inner work, but I wanted more #church. I wanted to be humbled and challenged. I wondered what else might be revealed if I continued to prostrate myself to Mother Nature. And she didn't disappoint.

I decided to look at this leg of the journey through a new lens. Literally. Photography had always been a passion of mine, one inspired by my dad. He had traveled the world with his Nikon and snapped the most exquisite scenes, often on his early-morning runs. An old clapboard schoolhouse shrouded in mist on the rugged northern coast of California; the ancient harbor of Antalya, Turkey, at dawn; and so many others. Several of his photos are framed and hung throughout my parents' house, each captioned and signed. I always admired his ability to capture his reverence for what was placed in his path in that moment. Nothing posed, filtered, or manipulated. Just beauty, reflected by the beholder.

I wanted that experience again. I used to obsess over my Leica X2, taking pride in the technical skill of an old-school manual machine, but it was too easy to get lazy with my iPhone—not to mention its many filtering apps—in France and New Zealand. Yes, the camera on the iPhone was progressively getting better, but, in my opinion, it's a far more intentional and creative experience when you can manually adjust aperture, shutter speed, and ISO. You get to determine exactly how you want to capture a particular scene, based on how you are uniquely seeing it, versus defaulting to the automated settings. It seemed a pretty apropos metaphor for how I was starting to live my life—intentional about speed, depth, and perspective in every moment. No more defaulting.

So I bought a gorgeous Sony a7R digital full-frame camera, and decided our first adventure together would be to the majestic Canadian Rockies: Banff, Lake Louise, and Jasper. Not only was it another destination on my bucket list, but Sevgi, aka the other Sylvester, happened to be living in Calgary, Alberta, the doorstep to this wonderland. It was a no-brainer. She and I made plans for a road trip in June when, of course, it would be perfect weather for hiking, glacier walking, and photographing the pristine turquoise mountain lakes—or so we thought.

Not exactly. We rocked up to Lake Louise in the midst of a full-blown snowstorm. Mother Nature must've gotten her J months mixed up. It was more January than June—the polar opposite of the wardrobes we had brought. Despite piling on nearly every layer we had, we were woefully underdressed. Our gloveless fingers froze just trying to hold our cameras. So we broke down and did that thing you try to avoid on any trip—we shopped for supplies at a hotel. We weren't staying right on Lake Louise, so the best/only option before frostbite set in was the ritzy Fairmont Chateau Lake

Louise a few hundred yards away. The cheapest pair of gloves was $75. (Having "Chateau" in your name apparently justifies a 250 percent retail markup.) As much as our shivering bodies wanted the comfort of cozy down parkas, we decided they weren't worth the price of a monthly mortgage on a small home. We purchased the gloves, summoned our hearty Minneapolis/Ottawa stock, and ventured out to take what ended up being some of the most sublime photographs of the entire trip. Because we embraced the beauty of the elements.

I was reminded of motorcycling again. Part of the je ne sais quoi of ridership (I was in Canada, so by law I had to say at least one thing in French, right?) is knowing that when you break out of the cage, aka the car, you need to be prepared for whatever may come. On a bike, you're exposed to, and at one with, the elements. Always. Hot, cold, rain, shine, sleet, or snow. I remember riding through pelting rain and hailstorms on the way to the famous Sturgis Rally in South Dakota one year (admittedly screaming like a banshee the entire time). Feeling the sunshine on my face on the other side was like a spiritual rebirth. It's the tightest companionship I've ever known. Riders can endure almost anything, because they know they're in it together. They'll support each other always. They are the ultimate tribe.

I realized that, off the bike, I was rediscovering the power of my own tribe—my blood family and my chosen family. My sister once gave me a wooden plaque that said, "You and I are sisters. Always remember that if you fall I will pick you up. Right after I finish laughing." That sounded about right. Family are the people who support you, but more important laugh with you—*and* at you.

Sevgi was as close to family as anyone I knew. Her word for it is "framily." When we finally made it up to Jasper from Lake Louise, she laughed hysterically when two longhorn rams almost cork-screwed me to death on the Old Fort Point hiking trail. I'll admit I might've gotten a little cocky with my photography, approaching two very wild animals for a close-up with a wide-angle lens. Especially when they decided to chase me across the plateau toward the edge of the cliff. I was sprinting for my life, hugging my new camera, and accepting once and for all: I am a city girl. I would be a goner on the first day of *Naked and Afraid*. Thankfully, the rams were just testing me, showing me who was boss. I was in their home, after all.

Note to self: Invest in a telephoto lens next time.

Minnesota, Italy, and Carmel—The Power of the Tribe

This humbled city girl returned to her natural habitat in late June. Ready to see a few friends and prep for the annual gathering of "the Chiefs"—the BFFs from Istanbul—on what we dubbed Lehto Island in the middle of Tyson Lake in northern Ontario, Canada. It was our Tribe Time, our traditional and highly anticipated off-the-grid escape with Sevgi, Didem, Markus, Luka, and any combination of partners/lovers/friends/family each year. No electricity or Wi-Fi or modern plumbing. Just blissful days of uninterrupted connection, conversation, music, backgammon, scrabble, reading, writing, hiking, paddleboarding, pedal boating, cooking, drinking, swimming, and saunaing (because, the Finnish). A reminder of the simple life, and of what really matters.

But I didn't get to take part that year.

Instead I got the call about my dad's stroke. As devastating as it was, I couldn't deny the divine timing. I happened to be home in Chicago, not on the other side of the world or working a full-time job, so I was ready to step up for my family—my blood tribe—after all these years. My eyes were wide open to the lessons of the Universe and, as you already know, my dad getting critically ill was like the Mega Millions lottery of lessons: We get one shot at this life.

Actually, my dad and I both got two.

As I've written, I spent the next six months with my mom and dad, dedicated to life itself, and what's possible when we push through the impossible. What you don't know is that I also took time out for myself. In the spirit of Soulbbatical, and to combat caregiver burnout, I took a couple of soul breaks from my dad's care to top up my own energy reserves and connect with old and new tribes.

The first was Sevgi's fiftieth birthday in Italy. We gathered the Chiefs at the most incredible Tuscan villa, in a tiny hilltop village called Belforte, to celebrate life and love. A majestic, one-hundred-year old, fifty-foot maritime pine stood tall and proud in the backyard, like a sentinel keeping watch over the villa. We were mesmerized and inspired by it. We called it the "Imagination Tree" because it became our muse—each of us felt an intense creative spark in its presence. We were writing, painting, composing, cooking, and dreaming in new ways. We even cocreated an Imagination Tree song one afternoon. With Markus on the guitar and everyone singing (more in homage than in harmony):

> We spent the days in your cool shadow
> And hot nights under your spell.
> Your roots were deep, and your branches proud
> And your wisdom was a well.
> You were as sharp as your needles,
> And as soft as your glow.
> It was like there was nothing
> That you didn't know.

Your silhouette stood strong
In the epic night's storm
Strokes of lightning illuminate
Your beautiful form.
High, high on the ridge,
Looking on green hills and golden fields
A hundred years, what have you seen?
What love, what loss, what still needs to heal?

Refrain:
Through the storms
And through the drought
You stood so tall
And knew what it was all about.

Chorus:
Imagination of mine.
Oh the tree that shines
Imagination of mine.
Oh, sweet as wine.

(Not likely to soar to the top of the Billboard Hot 100 if ever recorded, but a magical moment among friends nonetheless.)

Sitting under the spell of the Imagination Tree, I recalled my passion to rewrite the script of success. Deep in my soul, I knew success could look like joy and fulfillment, not misery and money. Especially after talking with my dad about shifting from living business to the business of living. The business of living is about creating a life you love because it's authentic, courageous, and on purpose.

It's about letting go of the stories and the shoulds and the armor, and being *you* in the world.

Then it rocked me like a soul bomb. I looked up at my brilliant tribe scattered across the lawn, each creating his or her own magic, and shouted my epiphany, "You guys! Soulbbatical isn't about taking a year off. It's a way of living. Where you choose to be Chief Soul Officer of your own life. Every damn day. I want to inspire and coach people to *live* this way. I want to show them what's possible when they liberate their soul. I have to share my story!"

Markus and Sevgi glanced at each other with knowing smiles before Markus said to me with equal parts love and conviction, "That's your mission, Chief. Make it happen."

And so it began—Soulbbatical the experience was becoming Soulbbatical the mission. The next month I took these ideas to a writing retreat in Carmel, California, run by Linda Sivertsen, author, Book Mama, and host of the *Beautiful Writers Podcast*. Linda and I and the four other gorgeous souls with whom I shared a home and some of the best meals of my life that week, became my new tribe and sounding board for the future.

At our first late-night live reading session, where you share work with the group for feedback, I read a couple of essays I'd written in New Zealand. They captured the essence of Soulbbatical and pieces of my story. When I finished, the room was dead quiet. I was terrified that no one wanted to tell me how awful it really was, that I had no business sitting in this room with these wildly talented writers, wasting everyone's precious time. My gremlins were raging.

Finally Linda broke the silence, "Honey, this is so much bigger than a book. This is a movement."

"And a business," chimed in Bronwyn, a successful communication and TED-talk coach and now podcast host.

"You need to be coaching this stuff, girlfriend," said Annis, a fellow corporate refugee turned coach, consultant, and writer.

I smiled and nodded. "I just said all of that to my tribe in Italy last month. This *is* my mission."

"Why don't you use the time here in Carmel to outline your vision, manifesto, and platform? The book will be a byproduct of what you create. The story will eventually write itself," Linda suggested. And she was right. It was time for me to think bigger.

I spent the next several days drafting and sharing my vision, a manifesto, a Soulbbatical glossary of terms, and more writing. I went with the intention of starting my book and walked away with the platform for Soulbbatical, the movement and business: coaching, global retreats, inspirational content, speaking gigs, and, one day, a book.

The Universe, of course, had other plans. Here I am sharing my story years before I thought I might. I swear you can't plan for this stuff. So, let's band together and stop trying. Let's relax into the reality that we can't even imagine the magnitude of what the Universe has in store for us if we trust and lean into the turn.

Are you with me?

This is where it gets really fun. I promise.

11.

LIVING SOULBBATICAL (FOR REAL)

First things first. How badly do you really want to change your life? You'll need to feel it in your bones, because it's going to take effort. You've had a front-row seat to my struggles and pain, and my commitment to change. You can't outsource this kind of work. (Believe me, if you could, I would have had it delivered with my groceries every week.) There's no hack to living your best life. Period.

We're a culture in perpetual search of shortcuts. Hacks are in vogue these days: beauty hacks, bio hacks, game hacks, dating hacks. Google delivers more than four hundred million results for the query "life hacks" alone. Houston, we have a problem.

I can wrap my head around hacking when it comes to finding MacGyver-worthy solutions for household chores, home projects, etc., but I get really suspicious when the concept expands into emotional and experiential realms. In my experience, the most profound breakthroughs come from doing the courageous-messy-uncomfortable-deep-sometimes-shitty work. Not from trying to find a bypass for more immediate gratification. Life is for living, not hacking.

Soulbbatical is not a quick and dirty undertaking. It's long and deep. (Hey, get your mind out of the gutter.) It could be your life's work, if you choose to make it so. And it's incredibly rewarding. I'll tell you this: the return on investment (ROI) on every dollar I've spent since making the choice to live my best life has (so far) been greater than any I delivered in my twenty-six-year business career. And I was pretty good at what I did.

Admittedly, I look at ROI a bit differently now. It's not simply about dollars returned on dollars invested. When you're in alignment with your soul's purpose, your whole relationship with money begins to shift. I can't possibly express it more eloquently than Lynne Twist does in *The Soul of Money: Transforming Your Relationship with Money and Life*:

> *Money moving in the direction of our highest commitments nourishes our world and ourselves. What you appreciate appreciates. When you make a difference with what you have, it expands. Collaboration creates prosperity. True abundance flows from enough; never from more. Money carries our intention. If we use it with integrity, then it carries integrity forward. Know the flow—take responsibility for the way your money moves in the world. Let your soul inform your money and your money express your soul.*

That quote blows my mind every time. *Let your money express your soul.* In my case, expressing my soul is about making courageous investments that will return joy, fulfillment, and impact. For example, in my first full year in business, I invested over sixty thousand dollars—money I was not yet making—in kick-ass coaches, community, and catharsis that would challenge me to play big. I had major skin in the game of life. It was edgy, but I trusted that the money would follow if I honored that sacred contract.

As my soul sister and fellow coach Demi explains it, money is simply another form of energy. It can be constraining or expansive; it's your choice how you want to relate to it. The very day I heard that, I penned this powerful commitment to myself: "From this day forward, I am investing in my relationship with money in the same loving way I am with my soul. Money will come *from* purpose and *with* ease." It's transformed how I think about my business and investments, and how effortlessly money flows to me now. What's fascinating, when you truly live this idea, is that money becomes a lagging indicator. Purpose and intention are the true leading indicators that you're on course. Perhaps this is a reminder not to let money prevent you from following your soul's purpose.

Willie G. Davidson, the reigning pope of motorcycling and grandson of one of the Harley-Davidson founders, once shared his design philosophy with me: "Form follows function, but both report to emotion." I love the simplicity and truth of that statement, so I adapted it as a mantra for Soulbbatical: "Intention follows purpose, but both report to soul." Staying connected to the wisdom of the soul is what creates the magic, just as emotion does for a Harley. It's not just a motorcycle, it's a profound experience. And so is your life.

From the day I left Linda Sivertsen's writing retreat in Carmel, my intentions for Soulbbatical were tattooed on my brain:

- Live my most soul-centered, authentic, and courageous life every day

- Create a powerful platform and movement to inspire others to do the same
- Serve my ass off to help liberate millions of other beautiful souls

I was going to become a Soulpreneur. The word made my whole body tingle. I was stepping out on my own for the first time in my life, at forty-eight—living proof that it's never too late. I felt that double-whammy of terror and excitement that inevitably means you're striding in the direction of growth. It feels wildly uncomfortable—like wearing your (non-stretch) skinny jeans to an indulgent Thanksgiving dinner. You're bursting at the seams, because you're no longer playing small. You can almost hear the Universe saying in that coy voice of hers, "Put on your stretchy pants, bitch. It's time to play BIG."

And, for the record, I didn't feel ready. I didn't feel ready when I left Harley (but I felt the pain and the void). I didn't feel ready to do the difficult inner work (but the Universe had other plans), and I certainly didn't feel ready to build my own freaking business from scratch (but I felt called).

It's a funny thing. We say the words "I don't feel ready" about all kinds of things—jobs, kids, relationships—but we're not actually feeling the feeling, just thinking the thought. The thought is our ego trying to save the day, to keep us safe and protected in a familiar sandbox because our nervous system can sense that we're approaching a new edge. Getting close to that edge causes even the best of us to "turtle," to snap back into our protective shell. The only way we overcome this reptilian response is to make intentional choices, and repeat them every day until our nervous system is retrained. It wasn't lost on me that my dad and I were rewiring our brains, and rebuilding our lives, at the same time.

. . .

My soul tribe in Carmel was right—Soulbbatical was a much bigger calling and concept. I had had similar ideas in the solitude of my soul in New Zealand, but I got scared. Like put-that-genie-back-in-the-bottle-and-launch-it-into-space scared. My gremlin voices were deafening: Who am I to teach people how to live? Who am I to preach about this made-up-word journey that I'm living (and still figuring out) in real time? I don't have all the answers. And I'm certainly not a "real" coach or entrepreneur.

Yeah, I was doing the thing that we humans do so well—we doubt our own power and experience, and concoct the most belittling possible stories in our heads. I had conveniently forgotten the part about being a trailblazer and courageous motherfucker with a quarter century of leadership experience under my leather-studded belt. Until it was reflected back to me, with so much love, by five gorgeous souls I had literally just met.

Who am I *not* to tell this story and spark this movement?

Who am I *not* to inspire and guide others to be authentic and courageous and compassionate?

That's exactly what I want to do for other people, I thought. I want to remind them of how powerful they really are. And show them how exponentially more powerful they can become, when living and leading and creating from the soul. And by people, I mean kindred spirits like you. Ready to embrace your best life.

The next few months post-Carmel were a juggling act of supporting my parents— and finally getting my dad to Florida—while figuring out how to design a life in service of my freshly inked intentions. I didn't even know where to start, so I reached out to coach friends, lawyer friends, design friends, and entrepreneur friends. I asked for guidance, recommendations, and help in bootstrapping together what would ultimately become Soulbbatical LLC. With little more than a legal entity, a logo, and a radical commitment to changing lives, I hung my virtual shingle in the world.

And I pulled in a six-figure income in the first year.

That probably makes it sound like I really had my shit together. Not so much. Here's the cringe-worthy truth: 90 percent of my revenue that first year was for marketing consulting work, not at all related to my mission of liberating souls. Truth. I tagged consulting onto my business card because it didn't feel as risky and woo-woo. I saw my value in the world entirely as a businesswoman, not as something eminently more important, yet less definable. And, hell, I was still in training to become a certified professional coach, so I didn't think of myself as a "real coach," despite the hundreds of people I had mentored and coached and developed in the corporate world (many of whom still thank me to this day for championing them and shining a light on their unique gifts). I was clearly operating from a place of fear, and wobbling something fierce.

Of course, the Universe had something to say about that. She wasn't going to let me abandon my mission and retreat to my old sandbox. No doubt she was watching me, crossing her arms and shaking her head as I took on a five-month, full-time contract to transform the marketing department of a struggling (but promising) retail brand. I had slipped right back into the cortisol culture of sixty-plus-hour weeks, being on demand seven-days a week, de-prioritizing self-care, and jumping on flights to and from the West Coast every other week. My hard-fought new boundaries had all but disappeared because I was afraid that living into my purpose meant I wouldn't be able to keep a roof over my head.

Fear had manifested the anti-Soulbbatical. Face palm.

The Universe let this lesson play out for a few months and then called bullshit on the whole charade. Actually, my body did. Just as in the bad old days, I got very ill. Only this time I understood exactly what was happening. I was way out of alignment with my intentions and my soul.

Not only was I not doing what I had set out to do, I was making terrible decisions in the process. I got on a plane to California with early-stage bronchitis for a week of meetings I convinced myself I couldn't miss. As if I was that invaluable. Within three days, I was in urgent care, breathing like a phlegmy Darth Vader, diagnosed with severe walking pneumonia. The doctor's orders were clear: super-strength antibiotics and bed rest for at least a week. No working, no flying. If I didn't comply, he assured me that the hospital was my next stop.

I have no idea how I kept my eyes open long enough to make it back to my hotel. I must've looked frightening as I shuffled and sputtered through the automated sliding glass entry doors of the Hampton Inn. The lovely (if not a bit freaked out) front desk attendant, who knew me as a frequent and generally lively guest, anxiously handed me two bottles of water and said, "Please call us if you need anything, Ms. Paxton."

I passed the next five days in a dark and spartan room, coming to terms with the choices I'd made. (And pondering whether I was going to die alone in a hotel with no room service.)

It was a moment of reckoning, for sure. In my delirium, I wondered if Soulbbatical was a modern-day hero's journey. It certainly seemed to have all the narrative elements I vaguely recalled from English lit classes in college: a call to adventure (check), crisis (check), challenges (check), death/rebirth (check), transformation (check), atonement (hmmmm), and return home (almost there). If so, was I experiencing the atonement phase right now? Was this my opportunity to release the fear that still held a surprisingly powerful grip on me? If I let go, could I return home and *finally* share the rewards with my people? Would I have the strength and courage to believe in myself and the impact I could have as a coach and movement-maker?

Six days later, on Easter Sunday, I boarded a plane for Chicago. The irony wasn't lost on me. My agnostic, recovering Catholic soul was experiencing its own resurrection. I was coming full circle, and ready to live Soulbbatical for real.

My consulting contract ended two months later, and the powerful choices began. Synchronicity took the wheel again. As painful as it was to turn down lucrative marketing consulting contracts—and believe me, I was getting coached off the ledge weekly—it created space in my life for nothing short of magic. I know that may sound over the top, but I can't explain it any other way. As soon as I focused my intention and attention on precisely what I wanted, I could feel my energy shift. The sandbags had been lifted, and my hot air balloon began to rise. Miracles were possible.

I could feel myself radiating an intense light of knowingness, rather than neediness. And with that came clients, community, and conversations I could never have imagined. I'm not saying it was easy, but when you start believing and creating, the momentum may surprise you. Suddenly I was attracting high-caliber coaching clients, and working within Fortune 100 companies, without a website or marketing plan. I was leveraging my old corporate network and growing an inspiring new one. I became a member of an iconic community for extraordinary leaders and coaches, and joined a coworking community for badass boss babes. I met my soul tribe in these places I never knew existed (and was initially intimidated to even set foot in!). People with shared values and a radical commitment to learning and growing and supporting one another in making the world a better place. Other soul-centered humans who instinctively understood and championed the mission of Soulbbatical; who thought I was brave, not crazy; who saw me for me.

I instantly connected with a former US Navy SEAL, kindred soul, and otherworldly healer, who looked at me our first day together and said, with piercing sincerity, "You *are* Soulbbatical, Shelley. Anything standing in your way needs to be released." He was spot on. I had been experiencing *myself* separate from my journey, and I was still tolerating toxicity in my life and in my body. I was unwittingly sabotaging my own potential. Christopher took my inner work to a level of freedom I didn't even know was possible. He quickly identified where a lifetime of accumulated stress was stored and, more important, where energy flow was completely blocked. He walked on my body—yep, that's part of the treatment—for nearly one hundred hours over several months to release the stress and reopen the constricted channels. It was some combination of torture, relief, agony, reckoning, and release. Through laughter and tears, we would chant, "Stress is a big fat bitch."

His work also demanded that I clean up my diet so I said sayonara to caffeine, alcohol, refined sugar, and most carbohydrates, in favor of a more conscious relationship with my body and soul; one that allowed me to be fully present and in tune with my needs and desires. It was time to leave decades of self-sabotage and avoidance and numbing in the dust.

Within months, I was resonating at energetic frequencies that could power a lighthouse.

And people felt it. I became a magnet for the things I wanted to create in the world. One of the dreams I had articulated in Carmel was to combine my passions for coaching and travel. To create deeply transformative experiences for clients, similar to what I had experienced myself in France and New Zealand. I had set my intentions but didn't feel ready to create one yet (yep, that old chestnut). And then a nudge from the Universe: Nathan, a friend and fellow coach, challenged me to colead my very first retreat with him in Norway, above the Arctic Circle and under the northern lights. His argument was a heaping spoonful of my own medicine: If not now, when?

We pulled off retreat planning and sales in a few short months, and sold out. It was a profound adventure—holding space for, and connecting deeply with, seven other souls willing to be vulnerable and courageous in service of creating an extraordinary life. It was as close as I've ever come to a true religious experience. And to understanding the power of intention and action.

After the retreat, my renewed sense of conviction gave me the courage to apply for high-profile programs with two members of my personal board of directors: Seth Godin and Brené Brown. To be clear, it's a virtual board that they don't even know they're on, but it serves to keep me inspired and on purpose. In my opinion, their work is the high-water mark for creating authentic impact in the world, alongside the other members I've hand-selected: Oprah, Arianna Huffington, Anthony Bourdain (RIP), Michelle Obama, and Tina Fey. For the old me, putting myself or my work out there in the early stages would've been a total no-go. I would've filed any ambitious opportunity under "Fuck it. Not gonna happen, so why bother?" But my new mantra was "Do it anyway." Do it in spite of the fear. Do it to push through the resistance. Do it because it matters. Do it because showing your work (even the messy bits) creates opportunity and connection.

So I did it. And got a 50 percent hit rate on the first round. (I'll take that any day.) Brené decided to take a chance on me for her Dare to Lead training program in 2019. Meeting her was like how she describes meeting Oprah and Dr. Maya Angelou: heart-pounding, knee-buckling, and life-altering. (For the record, Oprah, you're next on my list!)

I got the Brené news the day after I found myself in conversations with Simon & Schuster about the opportunity to share this story with the world. So many years before I expected to be "out there." Definitely before I was ready. Honestly, I thought I had to have it all figured out, and beautifully packaged, to be sharing these very words with you. How wrong I was. Apparently all I had to be was vulnerable enough to be seen on my journey, and share my experiences openly. The irony is that this book connects back to the consulting misstep. It's a reminder that in every failure, there's a gift. For me, it was meeting one person, in particular, who watched me stumble, helped me up, and reminded me of my mission in this world. The Soulbbatical mission I had passionately and vulnerably shared with him over many dinners in California. That same person later ended up at Simon & Schuster.

Life was unfolding as a series of beautiful synchronicities. It may sound like I'm oversimplifying it, but that's exactly how it happened. And it wasn't a coincidence (I don't believe in coincidences). I know in the fiber of my soul that the secret sauce was a combination of energy, courage, intention, gratitude, and focus. And, of course, trusting that I was exactly where I was supposed to be, every step of the way. Vishen Lakhiani, founder of Mindvalley, coined the brilliant phrase "bending reality" to describe the act of accelerating synchronicities and "luck" in life. (There's an impressive formula behind it if you want to dig deeper.) That's exactly what I was doing—I was bending my own reality into exactly what I wanted it to be. And so can you.

You don't need titles or certificates or wealth. You need enough vision, courage, and conviction to push through the fear. The fear never goes away. It's present even as I'm typing these words. Because with every stride (and keystroke) forward, I'm approaching a new edge that feels even more terrifying. I'm letting more of Shelley Paxton be seen in the world. That's the way it goes when we decide to play big. So bring on the stretchy pants. I'll have the bottomless buffet of synchronicity, please.

I could almost hear the Universe sigh under her breath and mutter, "I told you so."

Yes, you did. You led a horse to water, and she finally drank.

Actually, she's still drinking. Let me be very clear, this is not a conventional success story in the way that we're used to seeing them served up in the media—tied to mind-blowing monetary results, sexy awards, and/or bazillions of likes-views-followers. It is, however, a decades-in-the-making-and-still-growing platform celebrating soul success. Success *with* fulfillment and impact. By now you know how I love to invent words—can we make "Soul-cess" a thing, and measure it against the yardsticks of authenticity, courage, fulfillment, and compassion (for ourselves and each other)? What do you think? I'd love some company.

The reality is that I wasn't sure how to get this right. I was just doing it one step at a time. Falling on my face, picking myself up, and getting better at pausing and reflecting. In hindsight, I guess that's one of my greatest strengths: tenacity in service of my intuition. Only now am I able to piece together the story and share it, unvarnished, with you. My hope is that the unscriptedness adds to the authenticity and inspiration. This is as real (and real time) as it gets.

I have no idea how this story ends. I'm still learning as I connect every thought in this book. Actually, writing this was one of the hardest things I've ever done; harder than leaving Harley-Davidson for sure. This process challenged my notion of Soulbbatical as I was simultaneously living and writing it. It was meta mindfuckery of the highest order to realize that Soulbbatical is constantly evolving. I'm a student of its principles every day—and always will be. I only know that I'm showing up, being the most courageous soul I can be, one day at a time.

I invite you to do the same.

12.

SPARKING A MOVEMENT

From the outside in, I may look like a new breed of soul revolutionary. From the inside out, I feel more like a revolutionary soul. And my goal is to spark a movement around authentic and courageous living. More of us creating lives we love, and radiating that energy and joy into the world. I like to think that a collective choice to rebel *for* fulfillment could summon the power we need to yank this country out of its malaise. Or at least initiate the wave of change.

When I look around, I see a lot of overstressed, overscheduled, overweight, and overmedicated people in the United States. More than one in three people struggle with unhappiness, major depression rates are rising, and suicide rates have increased 33 percent in the past twenty years alone. We're overachieving on all the wrong measures; winning accolades and bragging rights for tolerating, numbing, suffering, and checking out completely; for living in conflict with our souls and at war with our bodies.

It's time to stop the madness.

Someone once said to me about meditation, "If you can't find ten minutes, then you probably need three hours." Boom. A soul bomb, for sure. It made me wonder where else in my life I was applying that same shortsighted logic—sacrificing *being* for *doing*. Sure enough, I caught myself claiming to not have time for workouts, playing, creating, stillness, and so much more, because I was too busy hustling for my worth (as Brené would say). Can you relate? Are you finally ready to tell the busy-ness, the should-ing, and the not-enough-ness to go to hell?

Awesome. Let's do it.

Remember the mission I declared way back in the introduction? I said I want to liberate a billion souls. It's a massive number, but not an impossible one to reach if we do this together. I want Soulbbatical to live well beyond me, and my time on this planet. I believe it's the next phase of our evolution as a culture—more people desiring to live in alignment with their souls, and creating lives and businesses rooted in meaning and fulfillment. You can already feel and see it in the outbursts of civil activism and peaceful protests, in the beautiful celebrations of self-identity and expression, and in the standing up for (or kneeling down for) our truths and values. Living proof that authenticity is the truest form of rebellion.

As I was finishing this book, I lost a long-time friend and mentor to ALS (Lou Gehrig's disease)—just over a year after her initial diagnosis. Janet was sixty-one years young and still doing what set her soul on fire. Even while her body was failing her fast, she stayed committed to developing leaders of the future at Omnicom, and championing women in leadership everywhere. And, naturally, she became an outspoken advocate and fund-raiser for Project ALS. I loved Janet for so many reasons, and especially because she always followed her soul, channeled her charisma, and made an impact everywhere she showed up. She was a model for radical self-care, which made the devastating diagnosis seem that much crueler. Her passing is not only another piercing reminder that life is too short, but also that each of us has the opportunity to *live* a legacy. What do you want yours to be?

Seriously, if you knew this was going to be your last month, or year, on the planet, what would you do differently? Who knows where we are in the inevitable mortal countdown and yet so many of us continue to delay joy and fulfillment. Not to get all Grim Reaper, but we need to wake the fuck up, people! Forever is a fairy tale.

Tomorrow is a gift, not a guarantee.

The world needs more of us, like Janet, living into our fullest potential, leading courageously, and making a difference with every passing day. More of us "bending reality" (to recall Vishen Lakhiani) in service of our soul's passion and purpose. And more of us acting as the Chief Soul Officer of our own lives.

I'm inviting you to do exactly this. Christen yourself Chief Soul Officer in this moment. Take on the title. Sink into it. Feel the deep sense of responsibility it carries to know and nourish your soul. Get lost in the exploration of what it brings up.

What is it saying to you?

What is it craving?

What scares you?

What excites you?

What surprises you?

What inspires you?

What makes you wish you'd never picked up this book in the first place?

I'm only half-joking with that last question. Assuming the weighty title of Chief Soul Officer is kind of like letting the genie out of the bottle (the same one I told you I initially wanted to shove back in and rocket into space). There's no turning back once you've connected with your truest self. In pilot speak, you've reached the point of no return. Just sayin'.

Is your head ready to explode right now? I get it. Our minds can be nefarious creatures that feed us a whole bunch of malarkey to protect us from our truth. So, as difficult as this may seem in the moment, bear with me. There's light at the end of the tunnel.

You know how some products come with the warning label "Some assembly required"? Well, you're in luck. Nothing to assemble here—you were born with everything you need for this journey. You simply have to access and trust it. I want the Soulbbatical label to say, "Courage required. Confidence optional." As I've said before, confidence is the *result* of taking action and moving in a direction that feels right to you. Please don't wait for it—you'll miss life-changing opportunities if you do. Throughout my life, people have asked me, "Where do you get all your confidence from?" The truth is that, while my parents did their best to inspire it in me, I wasn't naturally born with any more confidence than you were. Instead, my secret weapon became courage. I got really good at pushing through fear once I realized that it was always going to be the nasty troll standing between me and what I really wanted. Soul versus Troll is no contest—unless you choose to hand over your power. (Please don't.)

I love what Marie Forleo says in *Everything Is Figureoutable*: "There can be no significant change in the world unless we first have the courage to change ourselves." Hell yes, sister! Can we all agree to that?

Let's Talk Purpose

I struggle with the word "purpose" because it feels overused, not to mention lofty and intimidating. It can send the best of us into a spin cycle of overwhelm. Believe me, I spent decades trying to nail down my elusive "why." I always believed that it had to be some epic statement that would rock the world and instantly change my life. And that, my friends, was exactly the problem. Purpose doesn't live in your head; it resides in your soul. Connecting with it is about embracing intuition over intellect. Intuition is that little voice inside you. You know, the one that you shush a lot, because it's often inconvenient? I'm telling you, listening to it is a game changer. It will shine a far more brilliant light on your purpose than some buzzword bingo statement written to satisfy your ego.

Purpose can be many things. It can be a passion. It can be a kernel of curiosity. It can be an unrequited need. It's often related to what you loved doing most as a kid, and maybe even still can't get enough of as an adult. What are you so passionate about that you lose track of time when you do it? What brings you unparalleled joy? And how do you share that gift with others?

One example that gives me goose bumps is from Nick Craig, founder of the Core Leadership Institute and author of *Leading from Purpose*. Nick inspires leaders to discover their purpose in order to lead more authentically. His genius is coaching leaders live, to tease out the stories that inform their "why." I'll never forget watching a video of Nick coaching a senior executive with questions that powerfully connected her to her favorite childhood memories (going on new adventures) and her greatest passion (skydiving). The combination revealing a soulful articulation of her purpose: "I help others to soar and create new adventures in their lives."

We all have something like this inside of us.

I'm not claiming to be an authority on purpose. My goal is simply to make the concept feel more accessible and less mystical—based on my own experience fumbling around in the dark, groping for the light switch. Start from whatever sparks the movement in you. Maybe you'll even be inspired enough to spend time with the questions at the end of this section. I double dare you.

So, let's start by calling bullshit on some of the myths that clutter the path to purpose:

Myth #1: We create our own purpose.

Quite the contrary. Purpose isn't an intellectual exercise; it's a soul story that's revealed or discovered. It's a powerful force that exists deep inside of us already. It's the unique magic that we have to share with the world—and the reason we're one of the miracles on this planet today. (Remember, no coincidences.)

The key to understanding it is connecting with ourselves and paying attention to what we love to do, what we are most passionate about, what change we want to see (and be) in the world. This is rarely a lightning bolt epiphany. The discovery comes as we spend time getting to know ourselves and exploring our values and gifts. Peeling back one layer at a time and getting curious about where it takes us. Trust the process—the scarier it feels, the closer you are to a breakthrough.

As you know, when I started this journey, I had achieved pretty amazing success by most standards, and, yet I still felt like I had only mastered the success part of successful. I didn't feel "ful"—or fulfilled—at all. In the beginning, I was in search of my soul, afraid I'd lost touch with it for good and hopeful that it might be the portal to purpose (or at least something more meaningful). I certainly didn't have a plan. I was living breadcrumb-to-breadcrumb, being transported on the wings of synchronicity from France to New Zealand to California to Canada. But your journey doesn't have to involve travel. Only trust. Trust in your intuition, the voice of your soul. We pay the price when we don't listen to that voice. And we discover possibilities when we do. Following my intuition led me down this path to liberate souls and spark a movement.

Myth #2: Purpose has to be an earth-shattering idea.

I think this is the one that trips us up most often. Like I said earlier, I thought my purpose had to be worthy of global headlines. That's a lot of unnecessary (and unhelpful) pressure. As a friend of mine says, there is little-p purpose—what you feel called to do day to day/week to week/month to month—and big-P Purpose, a bigger mission that guides all your actions. The beauty (and relief) is that these two forces aren't mutually exclusive; they coexist. Little-p passions may even lead you to your big-P Purpose, if you simply keep taking steps toward what brings *you* joy day after day. Forging your own path—not following someone else's.

As you know, I spent a lot of my life in seeking mode. I wasn't able to articulate a purpose until the end of my initial Soulbbatical, but I was always clear on my passion for travel and writing and photography. Those passions eventually led me to my purpose—once I started listening to my soul instead of the script in my head. So, while you don't have to have a perfectly articulated purpose, I invite you to get in touch with what really drives you, in its simplest form. Your soul has a story, and your story is your purpose. You just may have to sit still long enough to hear it.

And, don't be surprised if what you hear sounds simple. Actually, don't judge it at all. It's yours. Own it. We're shooting for earnest, not earth-shattering.

Myth #3: Purpose is not for profit.

I've heard people swat away the notion of purpose like a pesky mosquito, based on one single misconception: "You can't make a living following your purpose." But how true is that, really? How much of that is fear speaking? How much may it cost you to continue crouching behind those limiting beliefs? Language matters. We often use words like "can't," "should," and "have to" to relinquish responsibility for the choices we're making (or not). There's nothing wrong with saying, "I won't make a living following my purpose [or passion]." It simply means you're not ready or willing to prioritize it or put it into action. Just be honest with yourself. (That's the code of a Chief Soul Officer.)

While we're having this little truth sesh, let's also get real about how many wildly successful businesses have been founded on purpose, from a passion to do better/be better/look better/feel better. A few of my personal favorites are Tom's, Spanx, Beautycounter, and Mindvalley University. These companies were started in someone's soul—some as side hustles, others as going-for-broke ventures, but all with the courageous conviction of "I can." You know what they say—write the book you need to read, create the product or service you want to buy, and/or spark the change you want to see.

Now, I'm not saying you *have* to make a living following your purpose, but wouldn't it be insanely fulfilling if it worked out that way? If you embodied your purpose every day of your life, whether working for a company with a shared mission and similar values or starting a company of your own? (Asking for a friend.)

Myth #4: You have only one purpose.

Nope. Purpose is not a one-and-done kind of deal, nor is it forever etched in stone once you've landed on something that feels meaningful. In fact, it's far more likely that your purpose will evolve over time. (Hell, it might even lead you to discover multiple purposes in your lifetime. There's no rule or limit.) As Jay Shetty, former monk and host of the popular *On Purpose* podcast, says so eloquently, "Give your purpose the space to grow, change, and deepen." That means giving yourself permission to slow down, explore, and check in as often as you need. Feel whether you're heading in the right direction or whether you need to course-correct. Stay flexible and open to what might present itself along the way. The only Waze app for this trip is your soul.

I have to admit that I'm buzzing about the possibility of my current purpose—"liberating souls"—deepening, evolving, or somehow paving the way to something(s) even more profound. That feels like exactly the kind of journey I want to be on. Are you with me?

Ultimately, purpose is personal, and one of the best ways to discover yours is to spend quiet time alone, tuning in to that inner voice. Even if you can only set aside a couple of hours a week right now, I challenge you to do it. And to commit to being uninterruptable—devices off, in a private space or out in nature.

If you haven't practiced this before, it's going to feel super awkward and uncomfortable at first. It did for me. I remember running my to-do list, planning my next meal, and ranking the sexiness of the *Game of Thrones* cast in my mind, until I allowed myself to settle in deeper. You may even start by asking yourself these simple yet profound questions—"Where am I not being honest with myself?" or "What do I know to be true?" or any of the questions from the "Soul Search" reflection sections in this book—over and over again, until the answers evoke a visceral reaction. That's a good sign that you're getting somewhere. When I uncover nuggets of truth, my body tingles, my gut feels warm, and my eyes often water. Do you know what clarity and knowing feel like for you?

I can't predict what you'll discover, but I know one thing for certain. This reflection time will become so sacred that you'll not only crave it, you'll defend it with your life. And you'll be inspired to create more of it. It's the wellspring for everything this book holds dear: authenticity, courage, purpose, self-compassion, and fulfillment.

Making Soulbbatical Your Own

So, you're Chief Soul Officer of your own life, amped up on the commitment to nurture your soul, now what? I'm sure some of you are still thinking, *How the hell can I make this work in* my *life?* As I've said before, Soulbbatical is not one-size-fits-all, and it certainly doesn't mean you have to walk away from your career. There are so many different ways to approach this concept.

Whether you're at a Fortune 500 company, a start-up, at home, or out on your own, the principles of Soulbbatical can help you to discover and create your best life. Exactly how that happens—and how far you want to take it—is entirely up to you. You can take tiny steps toward bringing more soulfulness into your life, you can jump straight into an inside-out gut rehab like I did, or find something just a little bit edgy in between. It's a question only you can answer: What does greater soul-fillment look like for you? What is your soul craving? What is calling you to play so big you terrify yourself?

I've said this before, but I think it bears repeating. (My marketing training says we need to hear a message seven times for it to take hold. My mom would argue that stubborn people like me probably need a few more.) Soulbbatical is not a one-off escape or phenomenon (though it can certainly start that way). It's a way of being that will shift your entire world if you lean into it. And, remember, you don't have to know exactly where you're headed (most of us don't).

You simply have to trust that little voice, or that persistent tingle inside of you, and take the next right step. And the next right step after that. It's like driving in fog with your low beams on—slow and steady progress until the horizon becomes clear.

I invite you to make the concept of Soulbbatical your own. The possibilities are as infinite as the potential of each one of us, but here are three options to get your soul primed:

Soul Steps: Making Some Fundamental Changes

All change starts with tiny steps in the direction you want to head. Dan Sullivan, cofounder of Strategic Coach, teaches us to think about a long-term vision (like a twenty-five-year plan) in terms of the next ninety days. That's one percent of twenty-five years. I don't know about you, but I'm not wired to think about things that far out. Three months feels eminently less overwhelming, right? This is a way to ease into it—and to ensure that you're topping up your Soul Fuel on a regular basis. I can guarantee that the more soul-filled you feel, the more fiercely you will fight for your boundaries. And the more of this life you'll want to create.

So, here are some ways to dip your toe into more soulful living. Think about these in the context of what you're willing to create for yourself in the next three months (or more, if you're feeling ambitious):

Practice a morning routine that sets you up for success the rest of the day. What are the activities that catalyze the most energetic and productive day possible (and minimize self-sabotage)? Is it meditation, journaling, exercise, quiet time, gratitude and intention setting, and/or healthy eating? A biggie for me was gifting myself the time to start slow—or slower—instead of rushing into a cortisol crisis before 9:00 A.M. It sets the tone for how I want to approach life. Meditation, movement, and no screens before breakfast are nonnegotiables for me—or I'm already starting my day off on the wrong foot.

Make sleep a priority. Remember, you *can* sleep your way to the top (wink, wink). Arianna Huffington has been evangelizing that getting a good night's sleep is a superpower. The I'll-sleep-when-I'm-dead mentality so often linked to "success" ultimately leads to burnout, exhaustion, illness, or worse. The pivotal training element for the world's elite athletes is rest and recovery, so why should it be any different for the rest of us? You'll be amazed at the clarity and energy and creativity it opens up—not to mention that sleep is directly correlated to happiness. So, commit to a minimum of seven to eight hours of sleep per night. The other stuff can wait (for real).

Schedule a date night with yourself once a week. Friends optional. Partner optional. It's whatever you and your soul need in that moment. The time will be there for you. As Jay Shetty says, "Spontaneity comes from structure."

Create me-tings on your calendar every month before anything else fills up the space. Inviolable time for yourself—for stillness, journaling, meditating, reading, walking, or creating. Even if it's just an hour of alone time before anyone else in the house is awake. This is the opportunity to slow down, listen to yourself, and get really curious. (And if you tell me you don't have an hour, you know what I'm going to say, right? Perhaps you need three . . .)

Commit to "breaking out of the cage" more often. Try walking meetings, exercising outside, and getting out into nature for long weekends.

Uphold your boundaries. Say *no* to others and *yes* to yourself more often. Unapologetically creating space for you/your Soul Fuel. If, like me, you're more likely to say yes to commitments further into the future because they seem less real and more doable, then ask yourself this simple question that I learned from the wildly successful entrepreneur Derek Sivers: "What if this was happening two days from now? Would I still see it as a priority?" For most of us, a wobbly long-range "yes" for our future self quickly changes to a definitive near-term "no" for our current self. Another simple way to think about your commitments is in terms of Hell Yes, Hell No, and No For Now. Everything in your life can be sorted into these columns. As master coach Rich Litvin says, "There's no such thing as a 'Hell Maybe.'" So eliminate the maybes that are sucking your precious time and energy away. Get clear on your Hell Yeses.

Start pruning the biggest Soul Sucks from your life, especially the people who are draining your energy. Begin to form the soul tribe you want to live up to and into. By default, you'll be creating more space for what fuels you. And don't be surprised if you find yourself leveling up as a result. None of us can go it alone—and none of us should be bound by anything less than free will in any relationship. Not shame, guilt, humiliation, fear of rejection, perceived obligation, tenure, or blood ties. Be clear about the energy you want in your life.

Take intentional breaks during your workday. Our bodies and brains weren't built to sit in meetings and in front of screens for eight to ten hours straight (or longer). We need a break from the intensity to allow for integration of insights, learnings, and ideas. This is the bedrock of consciousness and creativity. Think of it like high intensity interval training—rounds of intense activity followed by less strenuous recovery activity. I like to call it a cycle of "rally and recovery"— and we can design our schedules this way. For example, I don't book coaching sessions back-to-back. I always allow for recovery and centering in between, usually fifteen to thirty minutes. So I rally for ninety minutes and recover for fifteen to thirty minutes. If you have meetings for longer stretches, simply build in longer recovery.

Create your vision for what an ideal day looks like. Keep in mind, this is an average weekday, not a dream holiday in Bora Bora. Start from a blank twenty-four-hour slate and first document the nonnegotiables that matter most to you, i.e., the "big rocks." For example, how much sleep do you want to get? How much time for family, partner, exercise, stillness, me-tings, work, social commitments, passion projects, etc.? I first did this exercise with my coach in 2015, and was blown away by the gap between my typical day and my ideal day. My priorities were upside down and inside out. I was living at the effect of my life, instead of creating it. How does yours look? What tiny steps do you want to take toward the ideal?

If you're feeling ambitious, design what your ideal year looks like. Start with intentional time off to recharge every quarter, and then layer in the big rocks from above. This will completely shift your perspective—and challenge you to be ruthless in prioritizing what's most important to you. It's the soul's checks-and-balances system, and the only way to honor it is to create clear boundaries—and to own your choices.

Breathe. Practice signaling to your body throughout the day that you're safe and calm by breathing deeply. I've learned the importance of this through meditation and, more recently, from Eric

Edmeades, founder of WildFit, a well-being program based on returning to the natural human diet. We think of optimal health as
simply a balance of diet and exercise. But it's so much more fundamental than that. It starts with the basics of air and water. Pause
throughout your day to take a deep breath in for five counts, hold
for five counts, and release for five counts. Repeat the sequence five
times. It keeps the cortisol rush at bay, so your body remains calm
and your consciousness expansive. (It helps combat lizard brain
when you get emotionally hooked, too! It's impossible to access your
greatness when you're in fight-or-flight mode.)

Do one thing a day that scares you. Yes, that thing. And that
other thing. All those things that your ego has tricked you into filing
under "one day" or "when I _____ (lose weight/have more money/
feel more confident/fill in the blank)" or "that's just plain ridiculous
for someone in their forties." Reach out to that person you've always
wanted to connect with, join that group that intimidates you, post
your first video on social media, write that first (or next) article and
publish it, request time off for that trip you've always wanted to
take, break up with that energy-vampire of a friend (you know the
one), outline the book you've always wanted to write, or champion
that edgy new project at work. I could go on and on. Suffice it to
say that if I can share my story with the world at fifty, I know you're
capable of putting yourself out there, too.

Soul Start: I'm Ready to Dive In

I've had so many people—friends and strangers—say to me, "I need
a Soulbbatical. How can I take one?" My response is always, "Create
one!" Seriously, ask for what you want and make it happen. Or, don't

ask and make it happen anyway. You're in charge. It's easier than you think. It doesn't have to last a year, either. In the Soulbbatical Stories below, you'll get the inside scoop on what my friend Gina did in a hundred days. It radically changed the trajectory of her life (and career).

I challenge you to set clear intentions—this is what makes a Soulbbatical different from a vacation. It's your time to re-source yourself and dig deeper. Approach your time away, even if it's only a few weeks, as a start to the lasting change that you want to bring to your day-to-day Soulbbatical life. Use this time to go into the cave and do the reflection, the meditation, and inner work that will begin to liberate your soul and illuminate your path. Pack this book, pass on the umbrella drinks, and get down to business. Take a long Soulbbatical (like I did) or do one of the following to jump-start a more soul-filling life:

Mini Soulbbaticals. Schedule these once a quarter, for at least a long weekend, or block longer stretches three times a year. Put these on your calendar before anything else. Uphold your boundaries and your commitments to yourself. Protect the time as if your life depends on it (because it does). This is what I do now that I'm running my business full-time. I've designed my life around having two months a year off for connection, compassion, and creation. Even while writing this book, I escaped to a friend's cottage on the water for weeks to commune with Mother Nature and ground myself in her divine truth. #church. What do you need most?

Retreats. I run Soulbbatical retreats every year (as do many other talented coaches and Soulpreneurs). They're essentially facilitated mini Soulbbaticals. We escape to fabulously inspirational places, go off the grid, and connect deeply with one another and ourselves. We nourish our souls and practice the inner work together. It's indescribable, until you experience it for yourself. You can find out more on my website, www.soulbbatical.com. (I'm also happy to talk about creating a custom Soulbbatical retreat for organizations or leadership teams. Shoot me an email at shelley@soulbbatical.com and let's co-create something transformational.)

Company-Supported Soul Time. Be the rebel who starts the conversation, if not the trend, at your company. Be the leader who requests and champions Soulbbaticals in your organization (like Mark-Hans and I did in our agency jobs way back when). Be the influencer who pioneers conversations around courageous culture and leadership, flexible schedules, morning autonomy, and rally and recovery scheduling as the norm. (Check out other examples in the Soul of Business section on pages 227–32.) What have you got to lose that's more important than your vitality and joy?

The Soul Monty: I'm All In on Living Soulbbatical

This is your time to go all in on the decision you've been wavering on. Time to live and lead more authentically, courageously, and on purpose, in every aspect of your life. Well, you've just read my journey, which seems as good a guide as any to getting started. Have you spent time diving into the "Soul Search" reflection sections of this book? What insights surfaced for you? What are you feeling inspired by but terrified of? Where are you ready to take action? I'd love to hear your breakthroughs, stories, and thoughts on how I can support you. Email me at shelley@soulbbatical.com.

Soulbbatical Stories

Like I said, this isn't a one-size-fits-all concept. So I want to share a few other Soulbbatical Stories that look different from mine. I'm hoping you'll find them thought provoking, if not downright inspiring. Honestly, there's no excuse for not creating your best life. Now.

Bye-Bye Burnout, Hello Dream Job

Gina, a senior sales executive at one of the world's largest technology companies, whom I had worked with in my Harley days, watched my Soulbbatical journey unfold in real time. It inspired her to want to do something similar for her own very personal reasons. She was exhausted and reaching burnout. Gina had been promoted to build a strategically important new group within the organization and then, in quick succession, lost her ex-husband, her grandma, and her mom. She didn't want to let the company down so she worked her ass off for three years to create a powerhouse team and impressive results, while compartmentalizing her grief. She tried to bypass feeling all the feels, until they caught up with her. So much so that she approached management and requested a hundred-day Soulbbatical. Sabbaticals, in general, were not standard issue at the company, but Gina had the courage to ask for what she wanted. She had no idea if her bosses would be supportive, but she knew she had to try. (Kind of like you-know-who when she was twenty-six years old.) Keep this in mind next time you think, *My company would* never *let me do that*. What's the worst thing that can happen? They say no and you're faced with a different set of choices. Or they say yes. All it takes is one person to start the conversation. That's exactly what Gina did.

Since she's a badass babe who prefers life on two wheels, she created an epic, mostly solo motorcycle ride cross-country from

California to New York—and back again. Oh, and she hopped across the Atlantic Ocean to do some riding in the Alps in between. Talk about *Zen and the Art of Motorcycle Philosophy*. She leaned in hard by spending time in nature, doing what she loves most, and listening to her soul. Along the way, she camped and created space for intentional reflection and healed some serious emotional trauma.

Halfway through the journey, she had two life-changing epiphanies: one work and one lifestyle. First, she realized that her work wasn't as fulfilling as she wanted it to be. She was great at sales, but it didn't light her up as much as creating and nurturing high-performing teams. She wondered what it would be like to have a greater impact on the organization as a whole; to work with leaders across the company to build more powerhouse teams and a thoughtful and courageous leadership culture. That was so clearly her passion and her zone of genius. Gina wrote a new job description for herself in her head—and put clear intentions into the Universe.

She also realized that she was craving a lifestyle change. She and her partner were based in San Francisco, but had purchased a small house in New Orleans, their favorite city and birthplace to their romance. They were in the midst of renovating it, feeling house poor, and only finding time to spend the occasional weekend down south to fuel their souls. Gina suddenly knew she wanted to downsize in the Bay Area and commit to spending at least 30 percent of the time in NOLA. She sent both her partner and the Universe little love notes.

One hundred and one days later, Gina returned home, with her authenticity, courage, and a new life vision in hand. She literally imagined her dream job at one of the most iconic technology companies, and it manifested into reality within weeks of her return. She was approached to lead progressive work in the organizational and cultural development space, across the entire company. It also allowed her the opportunity to train as a somatic coach (a body-led approach to transformative change) and impact thousands of leaders. In her view, she had radically shifted her own life and now wanted to pay it forward to others.

And she would do it from the Bay Area and NOLA and wherever else she and her partner decided to go. They both built flexibility into their work agreements.

Gina's advice: "Don't be afraid of what's in your heart. Make space to get to know yourself, get clear on what you want, and be fearless in pursuing it." (Don't mind me—I'm just over here doing my little hallelujah happy dance.)

If You Don't Try, You'll Never Know

Charlotte, her husband, and their tribe of four kids took a twelve-month family Soulbbatical before I ever invented the word. Charlotte was one of my college roommates. I always knew she was going to blaze trails. Back then we thought it would be as a senior executive in a global company; that had always been her dream. Then she met a Brit named Paul—on the back of an elephant in Thailand no less—and everything changed. They began traveling together and she knew immediately that life was going to be a bigger adventure than she could have ever imagined. She eventually married Paul, lived in multiple countries, and discovered that her true purpose was to usher four amazing children into this world, and show them how to live a life of authenticity and adventure.

Fast-forward to 2011, they were living in Ireland with four kids between the ages of three and a half and ten years old. Charlotte and Paul were feeling the suck of "same shit, different day" routines and a decades-long relationship gone stale. Paul was growing restless after ten years working in a big conglomerate, and unclear on his next career step. They didn't have massive savings stockpiled, but they knew they wanted to shake up their lives. For the sake of their marriage, their souls, and the well-being of their kids. Since meeting in Thailand, they had promised to live true to the philosophy of "work to live" yet, like so many of us, found themselves trapped in a vicious cycle of "live to work." They knew they had a window of opportunity to do something radical before their eldest entered middle school.

Paul left his corporate job with no safety net and they pulled the kids out of school for a year. Their intention was to create a beyond-the-classroom experience that would rival any traditional education. And to show their children firsthand what it feels like to do what you love and fuel your soul. Friends and family thought they were crazy, if not downright irresponsible. (Sound familiar?) But they went anyway, reasoning that they could always return home if it was a disaster. (It wasn't.)

They covered fifteen countries in twelve months, including six months in Latin America and a swing through New Zealand, Australia, and, of course, Thailand, where it all began. They lived on a shoestring budget by backpacking—each kid responsible for his/her own pack, even the youngest—and camping everywhere possible. Sharing their wanderlust with the kids forged tighter family bonds than ever before. They became "each other's everything" on the road, as Charlotte describes it, and "even the bad days were good" because they were giving their kids wings, perspective, and confidence. Not to mention a master class in resourcefulness and responsibility, amid the history and life lessons.

Paul returned to find a more fulfilling job and Charlotte was inspired to open a Pilates studio. Their eldest, now eighteen, has the confidence of an experienced adult and believes he can change the world. Their youngest, now eleven, is asking when they can go again.

Charlotte and Paul's advice: "You *can* do things that people tell you you can't. Don't look to others for acceptance or permission—do what feels right to you. If you don't try, you'll never know. Our Soulbbatical was the best thing we could've ever done for our kids and ourselves." (Cue Sister Sledge and "We Are Family"!)

Life Kept Real

Kurt was an executive at a Fortune 100 company when we met. His passion and talent were centered on user experience. Kurt was a genius when it came to understanding the customer and how to design a seamless and impactful journey from threshold to cash register. He loved to connect the soul of a space with the soul of a human. But he felt like that mission and passion were getting lost amid a company culture that celebrated politics, power, and productivity (at all cost). In his words, the experience was "sucking his soul."

I'll never forget our first conversation over dinner. The words he used were so hauntingly familiar. "Shelley, I'm losing myself. Every day I feel like I'm dying a little bit on the inside. I want time to reassess and reevaluate my life. I want space to rediscover myself. But I'm a husband and a father, so I can't make rash decisions about my career and paycheck."

I shared my own journey and reflections with him over several conversations. And coached him on some of the concepts in this book. Like so many of us, he knew exactly what his soul wanted him to do, but he feared jeopardizing his family's security. I helped him see clearly what the future was likely to be if he stayed the course—and what it could be if he embraced vulnerability and pushed through the fear. We worked to unpack what was standing in the way of joy and fulfillment, and to strip away the clunky armor that concealed his true self. Soon he started to believe (again) in his own power and potential—as a husband, father, creative, leader, and entrepreneur.

With a little financial planning, and a lot of courage, Kurt decided to make the leap to living Soulbbatical a couple of months later. His first order of business was to take some much needed time off to reconnect with himself and his family. One of the most powerful reminders of why he made the decision: He got to enjoy most of the summer with his daughter before she returned to college.

On Soulbbatical, he discovered that his purpose was, in fact, his passion. He followed his dream to open his own design consultancy, DKR (Design Kept Real). To end there would make for the perfectly packaged "happily ever after" story but I'm all about keeping it real too. While Kurt still leads DKR on the side, he made the decision to return to the corporate world after nearly a year away. He accepted a full-time executive role with a company that's aligned with his values and priorities. One that celebrates self-care, family time, and allows space for his passion projects—DKR Designs and a new men's lifestyle podcast called *The Bourbon Boys NC*, essentially four guys imbibing their favorite spirit and getting deep on learning how to live, love, play, and parent. Bourbon + Life for the common guy.

Last time I called to check in, Kurt was gushing with gratitude. "I've never loved my life more than I do right now. I'm relaxed, taking better care of myself, and open to the possibilities of where this all might lead. I'm focused on what matters most to me and my family—and having a lot of fun. Life's too short not to be." (Just in case you had that story in your head about walking away and never being employable again if it all goes to hell in a handbasket. Sometimes you do go back—on *your* terms.)

I could regale you with stories for hours, but I don't want to kill more trees. And I think you get the point. Suffice it to say I've had a few coaching clients leave their corporate jobs to pursue their dreams, but more often than not, Soulbbatical has been about doing the inner work that helps connect clients with their most authentic and powerful selves. And then bring that renewed energy to every aspect of their lives, including leadership. They find they are bringing more of themselves and their passion and gifts to work *because* they're carving out more time to nourish their souls. Some, like Kurt, are even finding new positions with companies that are more aligned with their values and purpose. Some, like Gina, are becoming a force for soulful change within their organizations. It's been incredible to witness.

Take a few minutes to reflect on those stories. What did you notice? How did you react to reading them? Were any of your gremlins waving the cautionary flag, trying to keep you safe from doing any of these crazy things?

Gina, Charlotte, and Kurt are really no different from you or me. They don't have trust funds or total financial freedom. They don't have superhuman strength or Ghostbusters-style weapons that render fear powerless in their presence. They don't have kinder, gentler gremlins in their heads. And they certainly don't have purposes bigger or better than yours or mine. They simply had the courage to flip the script to be aligned with their souls. And the conviction to push through many of the same limiting beliefs likely doing cartwheels in your head right now:

I can't because . . .

- I have kids
- I have a mortgage/tuition payments/insert favorite excuse here
- I have a spouse/partner
- I'm doing the responsible thing/what I should be doing
- I've invested all this time/energy into getting this far
- My company would freak out
- My clients would freak out
- My spouse/partner would freak out
- My family would freak out

The list is never-ending. And it always will be. Trust that Gina, Charlotte, and Kurt had an equally compelling litany of ~~reasons~~ excuses *not* to create the life—or the opportunity—they really wanted. And yet they chose to rebel *for* possibility. They chose to show up and be seen as their most authentic and courageous selves—family, mortgages and all. And not a single one regrets taking the leap.

So, I'll ask again, what's standing in your way?

The Soul of Business

Let's not only do this for ourselves, let's demand it of the organizations we lead and work within. Better yet, let's be the agents of change—the ripples that cause the wave. We're flipping the script in our own lives, so why not in business as well? Imagine sparking a movement that celebrates courageous leadership, radical self-care, and intentional downtime as the prerequisite for smart work.

The traditional narrative says work your ass off in order to earn time away. But then it often shames you for wanting to enjoy that time at all, let alone uninterrupted. I nearly fell out of my chair when I read this headline from a 2017 Glassdoor study: "The Average U.S. Employee Uses Barely Half of Their Annual Time Off." And, if I were a betting babe, I'd wager that, when those weary souls do take a break, they stay at least somewhat tethered to the mother ship. Most likely out of fear or cultural expectation, rather than any genuine indispensability. It's another layer of the undernourished, over-busy burnout pandemic. We're being conditioned to believe that we don't deserve time off, and that our mental, physical, and emotional health is somehow less important than our productivity. How can you even have productivity without energized, conscious, and inspired humans to do the producing?

News flash: YOU FUCKING CAN'T.

We have this all wrong. In so many companies, vacation is an afterthought; weekends are optional; and the urgent commands more attention than the important. Employees are in service of the culture, instead of the culture being in service of the employees.

Thinking about this got me flashing back to the early days of my advertising career. I remember being envious of the so-called creatives—the creative directors, art directors, and copywriters whose creative genius birthed brilliant new campaigns for our clients—and not just because they were the cool kids on the block, with offices full of toys and well-stocked mini fridges. The creatives were always having more fun than everyone else in the building because it was practically mandated in their job description. The founding fathers of modern advertising understood the importance of inspiration and play in unleashing the unconscious imagination. As David Ogilvy famously said, "When people aren't having any fun, they seldom produce good work."

What he was really saying is that sitting in meetings all day—or at a desk until midnight—isn't going to inspire the work. Not getting out into the world and exposing yourself to new thoughts and ideas is creative kryptonite. And to not allow all those provocative new inputs the time and space to seduce one another is almost criminal. Introduced in Matt Ridley's TED Talk "When Ideas Have Sex," this creative phenomenon has cheekily been called "idea sex."

I always wondered why this experience was reserved for the creatives. Aren't we all more valuable when we're feeling inspired and playful and expansive? Isn't that the true breeding ground for growth and creativity and innovation—no matter where you work?

There are some progressive companies leading the way, and we have the opportunity to influence so many more. I personally love the story of Stefan Sagmeister, cofounder of Sagmeister & Walsh design studio in NYC. Stefan was way ahead of the curve when he spoke on the TED stage in 2009. If you aren't familiar with his talk, here's the gist: Stefan and his partner close their studio for a full year every seven years in order to get inspired and refuel their creative souls. Their clients are in full support, because they ultimately reap the benefits. Stefan preaches about the restorative power of time off. His philosophy is to intersperse retirement years into working years, in order to make working years more creative, productive, and rewarding. We definitely agree that time off is like air and water for our souls—and that postponing the majority of it until retirement is silly.

In 2019, the Australian office of the global accounting firm Ernst & Young announced that they would be giving all employees up to twelve weeks of "life leave" every year to be used for travel, part-time work, personal growth, or nothing at all. The new policy was in response to employees demanding more flexible work environments and time to pursue their passions. Australians have long been on the forefront of working to live instead of living to work. They nailed the business of living as a culture long before my dad and I became enlightened that sunny day in Florida. Now I'm passionate about seeing programs like this expand to the Northern Hemisphere, where traditional sabbatical programs are typically only offered after ten to twenty years of service (if at all). Company sponsored Soulbbaticals could be the antidote to burnout and the answer to flagging engagement and creativity.

But it's not just about time off. We have the opportunity to bring radical self-care and conscious leadership to the C-suite agenda. Earlier I quoted Vishen Lakhiani, Founder of Mindvalley, a global organization whose mission it is to teach wisdom and transformational ideas that our traditional education systems ignore. I'll admit that I'm a huge fan and member of the community, not only because of the world-class content they create, but also because Vishen practices what he preaches. He has created an award-winning culture at Mindvalley HQ, in Kuala Lumpur, Malaysia, that serves the mind, body, and spirit of its employees. One of the most radical programs is what Vishen calls "morning autonomy"—company meetings don't start before 11:00 A.M., so employees can use the morning hours for family time, workouts, meditation, passion projects, service work, or whatever their souls desire. I think about how different my days in corporate might have been with that kind of flexibility and support.

There are also a handful of enlightened senior executives like Marc Benioff, CEO of Salesforce.com, pioneering cultures that serve the mindfulness of employees. Benioff has been a practitioner of meditation for two decades and, inspired by a conversation with a group of monks from France, decided to put meditation rooms on every floor of the Salesforce offices in San Francisco a few years ago. He believes there's a powerful connection between meditation and innovation—not least because some of the most innovative minds on the planet (think Steve Jobs, Larry Ellison, and Elon Musk) were/are big into meditation.

"There's a 'mindfulness' zone where employees can put their phones into a basket or whatever and go into an area where there's quiet," Benioff said at the Forbes CIO Summit in 2016. "I think this is really important to cultivating innovation in your company. You can go there and not have . . . chitchat going on in your mind for a few moments. That's more important today because we're in this always-on economy." The company also offers regular programmed meditations, walking meditations, and mindfulness instruction from experts and gurus. Even mindful meetings are a topic of conversation. This reinforces my conviction that true change starts at the top.

Lastly, I want to share a conceptual conversation I'm currently engaged in with a CEO in the health care space. He's concerned about burnout and turnover in one particular frontline nursing role in the company. He approached me about creating a company-sponsored Soulbbatical program that would provide employees in this position with paid time off to engage in a combination of mind/body/soul activities to re-source and reenergize. We're also talking about coaching support to help each employee develop a personalized recharge plan, understand how to prioritize their own self-care, learn stress- and energy-management strategies, and explore opportunities that allow each of them to return to work healthier, stronger, and better equipped to manage a high-stress role. Who knows where this will lead, but I'm thrilled that there are courageous executives out there willing to consider this kind of conscious investment. My vision is to expand this kind of program beyond a single role in a single company in a single industry. Burnout is an epidemic. Imagine that a certified Soulbbatical becomes a recognized and lauded life accomplishment. Now, that's progress.

My hope is that this is only the beginning of a new brand of Rebel Leadership. I would love to see the Soulbbatical philosophy be accepted and adopted by influential leaders, first for themselves and then for their organizations. It's a way of being that could transform cultures, industries, and the face of leadership. In fact, it could liberate the soul of business.

Imagine being part of a soul-centered community and movement in which more of us are creating lives and businesses we love, rooted in meaning and fulfillment; in which we're all risking to blossom, together.

This is where my book ends and yours begins.

Soul Search
Purpose

1. On a scale from 1 to 10, how on purpose (or with passion) are you living your life right now?

   > 1 = If leaving the house with two matching shoes every morning is purpose, I'm nailing it
   >
   > 10 = Got a sec to read my manifesto?
   >
   > 1 2 3 4 5 6 7 8 9 10

2. What lights up your soul more than anything else? Are you leaning into it or running away from it? Why?

3. Self-kindness and mindfulness are two crucial elements of self-compassion (as defined by Dr. Kristin Neff). Knowing that, what are your body and mind crying out for more of—and less of—in your life? For example, sleep, quiet time, digital detox, exercise, time away, play, etc.

4. Where in your life are you speeding toward a destination while forgetting to savor and be present in the journey? What incredible experiences are you missing by not slowing down?

5. Practice your own version of the "Who Am I?" exercise. Write a list of your innate qualities, characteristics, and strengths with "I am" before each. (Reminder: these are *not* external titles, accomplishments, and awards. Those don't represent the essence of who you truly are.) If you're stumped, poll a group of friends, family, and colleagues. Ask them what unique gifts you bring into every room you enter and what draws people to you.

I am_____

I am_____

I am_____

I am_____

I am_____

I am_____

I am_____

I am_____

I am_____

I am_____

I AM ENOUGH.

I AM ENOUGH.

I AM ENOUGH.

I LOVE YOU, _____. [Write your name in the blank.]

6. Loving yourself is a prerequisite to becoming your best self. So, what's standing in the way of your loving and fully expressing yourself? Write each emotion/belief/thought on a separate piece

of paper with the statement "I release_____." Remember my little ceremony at Cape Reinga in New Zealand, where I let go of Corporate Shelley? Create your own ceremony to release what's no longer serving you. I recommend burning the statements in a fireplace, firepit, or favorite candle. Liberate and celebrate.

7. Who is on your personal board of directors? What does each of them represent to you?

8. What legacy do you want to *live*? What steps need to happen now in order for that to unfold? (Here's an exercise to stimulate your thinking: Imagine you're watching over your own end-of-life celebration. What are people saying? What was it about how you lived that inspired people? What are they not saying that you wish they would?)

9. What's calling you to play so big that you scare the shit out of yourself? What are you risking if you ignore it?

S.O.U.L. Process

After spending time reflecting on the questions above, choose one new insight or truth you want to take action on now and follow the S.O.U.L. process below. Use this for as many insights as you want. Lather, rinse, repeat.

S: **Show up.** Commit to having integrity with yourself. Stop hiding and playing safe. State aloud the new truth you want to create in service of your authentic self. (It often starts with "I am_____," "I will_____," or "I can_____.")

O: **Own it.** Repeat the truth again and again until you believe it's possible, and then accept responsibility for making it happen. Evict any competing stories and disempowering language (I can't/I should/I have to) from your mind.

U: **Unleash it.** Put clear intentions into the Universe. Share your truth with those who will support, inspire, and/or mentor you. Take one small step toward what you want to create, and witness the synchronicity that follows. The Universe opens one door at a time.

L: **Live it.** Create boundaries and make conscious choices in service of your new truth. Prioritize it. Get creative. Ditch the excuses. Live the idea of who you want to become, or what you want to create, *before you're ready*.

EPILOGUE

Fellow Rebel Soul, thank you for sticking with me to the end. I left my heart and soul on these pages. And more than a few tearstains on the original manuscript.

I've done my best to model everything I've been writing about—authenticity, courage, vulnerability, and commitment to purpose. While there was a bit of editing along the way—primarily to address my penchant for endlessly hyphenated phrases and general disregard for the traditional rules of grammar—this is my flesh and blood inked into history. The possibility of what this memoir-manifesto-guide-thingy will become feels exhilarating and uncertain. But, as Brené taught me, you can't be brave and certain at the same time. So, here's to bravery in living our stories, wherever they may take us.

I can imagine the hodgepodge of emotions you're experiencing after two-hundred-plus pages of narrative ranging from heartbreaking to hell-raising. It's a lot to process. My best advice is to simply experience it all. Sit with it. Journal about it. Meditate on it. Allow it time to integrate and percolate. This is the messy middle where the magic happens. Please don't hit the fast-forward button on your own development. Possibility demands patience.

My dad and I made a pact with each other that, as we entered the business-of-living chapter of our lives, we would practice the patience that had eluded us on the sprint to "success." While neither one of us is closing in on monk status anytime soon, we are experiencing the possibility and positivity that come with staying steadfast and calm. What's fascinating to me is that, with patience, the revelations are seemingly endless. Getting into a relationship with yourself and your soul is the gift that keeps on giving. Truly.

As I started writing this epilogue, I was confronted with a trio of truths that felt worthy of exploration:

1. Surrender leads to success (not defeat).

This sounds like heresy to most of us from the corporate world (and/or Viking lineage). We're warriors, right? We set big, hairy, audacious goals that celebrate our immense productivity (often at the expense of our health and sanity). But, in the end, our soul always knows what it wants, and it works on its own timeline.

Soulbbatical is about allowing our souls to guide us without our personalities, identities, or preconceived notions getting in the way. It's accepting that our souls are shepherding us toward the experiences we need to have and surrendering to the flow instead of hammering our way through.

This book was an epic lesson in surrender for me.

I attempted to apply a corporate-productivity strategy to a soul process while I was writing this book. Ironic, isn't it? In the early writing days, I set daily word-count goals, and then got wildly frustrated when the words eluded me or came up shy of expectation. I cursed the keyboard, shot eye darts at the screen, and seriously questioned my ability to write a book. I called Patti, my book coach, on many occasions and dramatically proclaimed that I was drowning in the quicksand of my own ineptitude.

Until I remembered my own mantras, took my own advice, and relished my own wisdom. I asked my soul what it needed in that moment. A walk on the beach? A palate-cleansing podcast? The nourishment of a good book? Lunch with an inspiring friend? A day or three away from writing in order to process and integrate all the goodness that was percolating?

I did all of those things—and more—in the times it felt most uncomfortable to walk away. The times when I felt so crazily far behind where I thought I was supposed to be. The times when I traveled to California exclusively to write (and suddenly couldn't). But, somehow, I was always on track. My soul was running this show, too. I was having the experiences I was meant to have. I was shedding the remnants of a corporate identity and learning to surrender.

Inevitably, I was rewarded with flow, an abundance of words and thoughts and new ideas that simply took time to incubate and journey from the source. You see, when you give your soul what it needs, it will deliver—though it might not look the way you thought it would.

So often we can't hear what wants to be heard, what so desperately wants to come through us, because we believe we can't do something or that it must look a certain way. We get stuck on the soundtrack in our heads instead of surrendering to the song in our souls.

This book is proof positive of what can happen when you change the playlist.

2. Old habits die hard AF.

I was writing about how foundational self-compassion and self-care are to Soulbbatical, and yet some days (okay, many days) I forgot to practice any of either. I replaced my once sacred morning routine with a quick meditation and half a pot of decaf coffee, then went straight to texts, emails, coaching, and writing. My pristine diet went to hell in a handbasket the closer I got to my demons and deadlines.

Reliving the heartache of several of the stories in this book sent me rebounding into the arms of my (comfort food) exes—wine, pizza, and every cheese imaginable (from lick-your-fingers-lowbrow pimento to slice-delicately-as-though-you're-not-going-to-eat-the-entire-wedge truffle). I was eating and drinking my emotions all over again. The Ninja of Numbing was back—or had she only been on holiday? Before I knew it, I had gained thirty pounds and lost about 30 percent of the thick-and-wavy hair I had once taken for granted. I looked like I was ready to give birth to a literal book baby. It was a physical reminder that I was out of integrity and defaulting to my old way of being. And an emotional reminder that this work is continuous; the gremlins don't magically disappear.

3. "S" bombs are more powerful than "F" bombs.

No, I'm not talking about the word "shit" (or any of my favorite derivatives thereof). I'm not referring only to the "soul bomb" wisdom sprinkled liberally on these pages like Himalayan sea salt on warm edamame. I'm realizing a fascinating pattern—that the essence of Soulbbatical is steeped in some powerful "S" words that surfaced again and again on my journey. Here are the ones I noticed most often; I wonder whether they might be next-generation messages emerging from my soul:

Surrender: See #1 above. I never understood the power of this when I lived in constant and exhausting warrior mode (pre-Soulbbatical). Now I'm practicing surrendering to my truth (I'm a writer), my heart (I'm open to love), my calling (I'm a liberator of souls), and the softer, more sensual, more feminine me that I've rebelled against my whole life (I'm a Goddess). And yes, I'm still a badass, too. I'm excited for what this new energy will bring to my relationships, work, and book two (yep, there will be another one).

Self-compassion: See #2 above. For decades, I was my own worst enemy in this arena—beating myself up, destroying my hard-fought progress, and speaking to myself like a worthless thug instead of a loving friend. In the "Chutes and Ladders" game of life, this was a long and dangerous chute that could send me back to square one with a single role of the dice. Now I more consciously practice Dr. Kristin Neff's three elements of self-compassion: self-kindness (versus judgment), common humanity (versus isolation), and mindfulness (versus over-identification). Here are a few of the mantras I use as needed: "This is what brave looks like," "I'm not alone," and "I'm simply observing these thoughts—they don't control me." #Progress.

Stewardship: I spent my entire corporate career stewarding iconic brands—often at the expense of the most important one: my soul. Let this sink in: Merriam-Webster's definition of stewardship is "the careful and responsible management of something entrusted to one's care." Tell me that doesn't sound like a rallying cry to actively care for our souls and to become responsible stewards of our soul's purpose. Who's with me?

Slowness: Remember the phrase "slow down to speed up" and the commitment to patience I mentioned above? Slowness is the X factor in awareness, purpose, ideas, creativity, meaningful connection, and so much more. Life is not a rush to the finish line, my rebel friends. Savor it.

Simplicity: I have a history of overcomplicating things. Soul-bbatical opened my eyes to the power of simplicity—in choosing what and who matters most, in getting clear on a few top values, in being who I am, in banishing drama from my life, in creating the space to be, in everything. Life is only as complicated as we choose to make it.

Synchronicity: I know, I use this word a lot. You may already be sick of it. But there's no other way to describe what happened to me on Soulbbatical than Carl Jung's theory of synchronicity, which tells us that events that have no causal relationship yet still seem to be related in a significant way are "meaningful coincidences." Yep— once I was brave enough to put one foot in front of the other, the Universe starting opening doors like an enthusiastic bellman at a fancy hotel.

Oh, who am I kidding? I still love a good poetic use of the "F" bomb (as you may have noticed). My mom probably has a little prayer about that, too.

Speaking of my parents, you may be wondering how everything worked out with my dad. As I wrote earlier, it's not lost on me that he and I both got second chances. For now, we celebrate his progress and work with his limitations. He can (sort of) walk and (sort of) talk, but his right arm remains stubbornly asleep, and he still can't read or write or grasp the concept of time—which leads to many hilarious (and sometimes heartbreaking) conversations. This one, which we had twice a week for the seven months I was writing the book, pretty much says it all:

> **Dad:** Oh! Hey, Shel! Are you done with that thing yet?
>
> **Me:** Are you talking about my book, Dad?
>
> **Dad:** Oh yeah. That thing. Haven't you been working on that for a long time?
>
> **Me:** Well, not *that* long. Writing a book takes time.
>
> **Dad:** But shouldn't you be done by now?

Me: I'll be done in August, Dad. And the actual book will be printed in January.

Dad: Oh, okay. [*Pause.*] But why is it taking you so long?

(Come to think of it, the hard-charging, overachieving Dad I once knew would likely have been asking me the exact same questions.)

And then one day, as the August deadline was bearing down on me and the telltale signs of stress were too glaring to hide over FaceTime, the conversation shifted. Dad asked me whether I was done with "that thing" yet, and my eyes sprang leaks. I told him that the finish line was so close I could taste it, and I was doing my best to walk across it, even if I could no longer run. Instead of the usual follow-up questions, he surprised me by responding, "I'm so proud of you. Most people wouldn't have gotten this far. They would have given up a long time ago. But you—you stuck with it. That's a big deal. And so is your story."

Holy lucidity, Batman. I had no idea that he even understood what I was doing. It was all the encouragement I needed to keep typing.

That wasn't the only poignant parental moment. I'll never forget my mom saying one night, on a recent visit to Florida, "We love you so much. We're sorry we didn't believe in your decision to leave Harley. It's so clear now how right that decision was. You're following your calling and helping so many others to do the same. We just didn't understand it at the time."

Apology accepted, of course.

I would rather receive a heartfelt apology from my parents about a chance I took than offer a regretful apology to my future self for one I didn't.

What do you want to say to your future self: "Thank God I did that!" or "I wish I would have . . ."?

You know the answer.

Listen to your soul.

Be courageous.

Your best life awaits you.

Now.

Soulfully,

Shelley

P.S.: I will be donating a portion of the proceeds from this book to the Life Is Priceless Foundation in honor of David Price and in support of the research and treatment of depression and suicide prevention.

ACKNOWLEDGMENTS

First and foremost, I want to acknowledge all the enlightened souls who read this book. Thank you for trusting me as your guide on this journey. I'm beyond excited to see each and every one of you unleash your infinite possibility in this world. That's a world I want to live in for a very long time.

To my incredible parents and one and only sister-BFF-fixer, Christy (aka Little Owen): We've been through a lot over the decades, but I'll take our family shit over anyone else's any day of the week. Love you all so much. Thank you for sticking with me even when you thought I'd lost my mind. (And, Dad, thanks for deciding to give life another shot. You are a beacon of resilience and perseverance for us all.)

To my Joint Chiefs Forever, Sevgi Demir, Didem Erbatur, and Markus Lehto, my chosen family: We'll be together in spirit always, in between adventures to Camp, Italy, London, Istanbul, and wherever else our souls are called. The three of you are my heart, my inspiration, and my reassurance that I'm never alone in this world. I'm so grateful the Universe brought us together in Istanbul those many years ago.

To my unwavering, wholehearted cheerleading squad across the pond, Dr. Mandy Lehto and Danielle Macleod: Mandy, you're not only one of the most brilliant minds I know, you're the poster child for curiosity, generosity, and creativity. I can't wait for the world to be introduced to your writing. Thank you for helping to perk up mine when I felt like I was running out of words (and steam). And, Danielle, the most remarkable and courageous woman I know, you showed me how writing this book could be easy (or at least easier than I was making it). Thank you for blazing trails for so many to follow. I'm infinitely grateful to call you both dear friends and wonderful wing-women on this journey.

To the best book coach ever, Patti M. Hall: The title "book coach" doesn't even begin to describe your immense talent and support. You were my champion, cheerleader, thread puller, memory prompter, co-conspirator, therapist, coach, editor, and, best of all, friend. I could never have done this without you. I'd still be on the first chapter (crying). Thank you from the depths of my heart and soul.

To Rich Litvin and the unparalleled 4PC community for the love, inspiration, support, coaching, and all-around badassery that gets me fired up. I love you all—Mandy, Teo, Christopher, Vicki, Luisa, Townsend, Catherine, Parissa, Hayden, David, Garrison, Niiamah, Alexis S., Alexis A., Monique, Wendy, Angela, Sarah, Erin, Matt, Varian, Laurie, and Jenny. A very special shout-out to Christopher Maher, who saw in me (and Soulbbatical) the potential that is still blossoming today; you helped me through the profound work of accessing my energetic potential by releasing the significant stress stored in my body. I can say without hesitation that I am finally authentically me. I have so much love and gratitude for you, Christopher.

To the rock-star team at Tiller Press for believing in me and my story. I knew I'd met my match when I learned about the vision for this rebel imprint within Simon & Schuster. Thank you, Liz, Theresa, Sam, Anja, Emily, Kate, Michael, Marlena, and so many others I have yet to meet. Special shout-outs to Sam Ford (for making it all happen), Emily Carleton (for being an incredibly supportive and collaborative editor), and Kate Davids (for guiding me so patiently in all things digital). Big love all around.

To the many like-minded souls who hosted me and my laptop on this journey: This book was, in many ways, started in New Zealand and then continued across Chicago, Santa Fe, LA, Naples, and the teeny-tiny lakefront hamlet of Oostburg, Wisconsin. Thank you to my hosts Bess and Gordon at Adrift and Richard and Vanessa at Driftwood Escapes in New Zealand; Janet and Julie at my favorite Airbnbs in LA; the warm and welcoming staff at Ten Thousand Waves resort in Santa Fe; and to my dear friends Julie and Bill for generously making their Oostburg cottage available to me so I could write on the water, my happy place. (Cheers to the gang at Il Ritrovo in Sheboygan, Wisconsin, who kept me fed and lubricated when I came out of my writing foxhole. Your authentic Neapolitan pizzas were well worth going off the rails for a few months!)

To Linda Sivertsen and the Carmel Writing retreat babes (Annis, Bronwyn, Claire, and Liz), who encouraged me to bring the bigger Soulbbatical vision to life. Thank you for the enthusiastic feedback and support. You've been with me in spirit on this entire journey.

To the "A" team in Chicago and beyond. (You all know who you are.) You can thank me later for not including any of our debaucherous "That Guy" stories in the book. Love you lushes.

To my courageous clients past, present, and future: I will forever be a champion of your power and possibility in this world. You're the reason I wake up with a smile every day. Thank you for being true to you.

To my courageous coaches past, present, and future: Thank you, Roberta, Morgan, Chris, and Rich for everything you've helped me to see in myself. Because of your support, I've been on a rocket ship these past few years.

To Gina, Charlotte, and Kurt for being brave enough to rewrite their own stories and allow me to share them here. Thank you.

To Mark-Hans, Shari, Kerri, Torie, and so many others who helped to shape the experience of Soulbbatical (the first and second time around): I'm forever indebted. You are in my heart and forever woven into the fabric of this story.

To my personal board of directors—Oprah Winfrey, Arianna Huffington, Brené Brown, Michelle Obama, Anthony Bourdain (RIP), and Tina Fey: You don't know me, but please know the immense gratitude I have for the high bar you've all set for living authentically, speaking your truth, and making a real difference in the world as a result. You are *my* soul guides. And standing beside you is a chorus of incredible humans from whom I draw inspiration every day, including Liz Gilbert, Seth Godin, Jay Shetty, Marie Forleo, Bozoma St. John, Lori Harder, Byron Katie, Vishen Lakhiani, Cheryl Strayed, Sara Blakely, Maria Popova, Amy Poehler, Amy Schumer, and so many more.

To Brené Brown: You are the brave, beautiful badass I want to live up to every day. Thank you for modeling wholehearted living, even (and especially) when it's really freaking hard. Training with you was an honor.

To my guardian angels Zoe, Moka, David, and Janet: Thank you for watching over me and reminding me how fleeting and precious life really is. You inspire me to play full out even when I'm quaking in my kickass boots.

To everyone else who called, texted, visited, and/or emailed to check in on my progress while writing: Thank you for all the love and support. I can finally say, "I'm fucking done!" What a wild ride. So grateful for the company.

To all the mix-ups, mistakes, wrong turns, falls, and failures along the way: Thank you for the learning and the lessons. Without them, I wouldn't be here.

And, finally, to the Universe: Your wisdom and powers continue to astound me. You have my trust and faith always.

ABOUT THE AUTHOR

Shelley Paxton is an author, speaker, and transformational coach. She spent twenty-six years as a highly regarded marketing and advertising executive stewarding some of the world's most iconic brands, including Harley-Davidson, Visa, McDonald's, and AOL. In 2016 she left the corporate world to become Chief Soul Officer of her life and, ultimately, her own company. She launched Soulbbatical with the mandate to liberate the souls of leaders and organizations by inspiring them to realize their greatest purpose and potential. As a certified professional coach, Shelley works with executives at Fortune 100 companies, and with fellow rebel-soul individuals and entrepreneurs. She is also a certified Dare to Lead Facilitator, part of Brené Brown's community. Shelley is based in Chicago (when she's not indulging her wanderlust). She's living her highest values of freedom, courage, and authenticity. And she's obsessed with the color orange.

www.soulbbatical.com

☺ **@soulbbatical**

🄵 **Soulbbatical Coaching**

1-13-2020